Religious Lite

Religious life

CONQUEST BY SUFFERING

Books by
HARVEY SEIFERT
Published by The Westminster Press ®

Conquest by Suffering:
The Process and Prospects of Nonviolent Resistance

Ethical Resources for International Relations
(Christian Perspectives on Social Problems)

CONQUEST BY SUFFERING

THE PROCESS
AND PROSPECTS
OF
NONVIOLENT RESISTANCE

by
Harvey Seifert

PHILADELPHIA

THE WESTMINSTER PRESS

PUBLISHED BY THE WESTMINSTER PRESS
PHILADELPHIA, PENNSYLVANIA ⑲

PRINTED IN THE UNITED STATES OF AMERICA

To
Carolyn, Mary Lois, and Linda Jean
who will inherit both our failures
and our conquests

CONTENTS

PREFACE

Thinking with our neighbor's mind is a common custom among us. Then he in turn thinks our thoughts, which have already reflected his. Consequently, all concerned are confirmed in conformity to the popular prejudice of the time. Even the mass media, with their sparkling new technological marvels, encourage this trade in secondhand, shopworn ideas. Such a perpetuation of past conclusions, on the level of average insight, is occurring at the very time that highly dynamic tensions demand novel thoughts, lifted to the level of brilliant analysis.

Working with our leaders' hands is another prevalent way of shifting responsibility. We leave major social action to those in authority in various social institutions. On complex matters in mass society we feel overwhelmed, helpless, and frustrated. Because we seem to count for so little, prevailing moods easily include meaninglessness and despair. Any fresh analysis of the problems of social change needs to provide handles to power which can be grasped by average citizens.

Nonviolent resistance, or nonviolent direct action, as it is sometimes called, has often offered to very ordinary persons a vehicle for dynamic change. The method has introduced a new form of power into a world plagued, on the one hand, with great resistances to change, and on the other hand, with increasingly destructive methods for forcing change. This form of nonviolence has raised again the question whether closer approximation to ethical and religious norms does not prove also to be more practically effective.

The method demands analysis also because of recent resurgences in its use. After centuries of history in many lands, nonviolent resistance has again in our time been adopted in widespread racial protests and colonial revolts. The spirit of Gandhi still lives in South Africa. The witness of Christian martyrs in ancient Rome is at least partially reflected also in modern Birmingham and Cleveland.

Enlisting the resources of ethics and the behavioral sciences, this book attempts to define nonviolent resistance more precisely than common usage has succeeded in doing. It traces the dynamics involved in the various stages of the social process. This is followed by an ethical evaluation in the light of the Christian perspective. The final chapters attempt a judgment concerning the effectiveness or usefulness of the method under a variety of contemporary circumstances. This also includes a discussion of important implications of the method for our more general programs of social witness.

During this research I have become deeply indebted to numerous individuals and to many university, public, and specialized libraries. Deserving special mention are the Hoover Institution on War, Revolution, and Peace at Stanford University, and the Swarthmore College Peace Collection. In addition to the steady cooperation of my own school and family, a grant from the American Association of Theological Schools made it possible to push this long-continued study to completion.

H. S.

School of Theology
Claremont, California

1

DISTINCTIVE FEATURES OF A NOVEL METHOD

On December 1, 1955, Mrs. Rosa Parks refused to move to a back seat on the segregated Cleveland Avenue bus in Montgomery, Alabama. By her refusal and subsequent arrest, this department store seamstress let loose a new force in American life. When four Negro college students, on February 2, 1960, continued to sit on stools in a Greensboro, North Carolina, variety store after being refused lunch counter service, they were using another version of that same force. One competent observer concludes, "No other method had ever achieved as much in so short a time as had these nonviolent protests."[1]

These campaigners for racial justice were resorting to the same method of social change used by Gandhi when he marched to the sea to make salt, or by his followers when they stood up to their necks in water demanding that the untouchables be allowed access to the Vykom temple road. These demonstrators were appealing to a social power similar to that released by early Christians in the arena or by later martyrs for their faith. The method ought to be particularly interesting to churchmen, for it has been a typical reaction of the faithful church under persecution.

Contemporary expressions in the United States have tended to remove from nonviolent resistance the esoteric or romantic veil that has associated the method with Indian mysticism or with faraway times and places. The method can no longer be thought of as irrelevant to Western industrial civilization or political forms. Indeed, when we begin seriously to search for illustrations we find a number of others in our own tradition. Quakers who broke the law by worshiping in the Massachusetts Bay Colony and woman suffragists who were imprisoned for picketing the White House had much in common with the contemporary children who marched down the streets of Birmingham, Alabama, with toothbrushes in their pockets to use when they went to jail.

There have been a surprising number of instances of nonviolent resistance in a variety of cultural situations around the world. These provide sociological data which is just beginning to be seriously studied. Most earlier writings tended to come from enthusiastic devotees. Their conclusions were untrustworthy because of their oversimplifications. Their materials were likely to be anecdotal, attempting to prove a conclusion by an illustration. More serious study may not allow us to share such an uncritical endorsement. Yet men of goodwill ought nevertheless to be actively probing any method that promises even so much as a suggestion for improving our usual procedures.

This is particularly true, since we are currently so poverty-stricken in methods for social change. From both sociological and ethical standpoints, we are experiencing a worldwide crisis in means. Ends are troublesome enough. Yet social scientists and churchmen have at least spent considerable time on them. We have formulated general social goals with a reasonable degree of adequacy. Thick books and continuous pronouncements are available to us, outlining changes considered necessary if we are to have world peace or racial equality or economic justice. Not nearly the same help is forthcoming on how those recommended changes can be brought about.

George Bernard Shaw is said to have remarked, "Though everybody nowadays seems to know the XYZ of everything, nobody knows the ABC of anything." Ours is an amazing ignorance about how to start in order to get where we want to go. Until quite recently, ethical and sociological leaders have not given the same thought to means or strategies as they have to goals. Even yet, churchmen seldom raise the question of methods except in the most general terms. Those who ought to be in the forefront of change often exhibit only a vague and naïve confidence in outmoded educational processes, or they appear to think that the mere denunciation of social evil discharges them from responsibility for patient, realistic support for social good. The result of our general neglect is a shocking lack of critical understanding of means at the very time when we desperately need more effective ways for reaching even proximate goals.

For one thing, on the international level our need for more effective methods has become crucial because of the destructiveness of modern war. We dare not dawdle over the project of installing a permanent successor to atomic attack. In a nuclear age we must find some way to win our victories without violence. In the internal affairs of nations, we also require more adequate methods of social change. Ours is an era of rapid social change. The future of nations depends upon their ability to accelerate social progress more rapidly than those with whom they are in competitive coexistence. The preservation of democracy now hangs heavily on the possibility of combining rapid social change with individual liberty. Can public opinion in free nations change rapidly enough and in orderly enough fashion to support the adaptations and alterations necessary in a swiftly moving world? It is not at all clear that this can be accomplished with the means now at hand. The situation is especially problematical wherever there are firmly entrenched vested interests or centralized controls by resisting power elites.

Even under slower-paced circumstances the social progress of democracies has often given the appearance of "muddling through." Now new nations of the world demand a considerably more rapid development of opportunity than has emerged from our past actions toward them. The realities of global interdependence are such that powerful nations anywhere are immediately involved in crisis everywhere. The necessities of policy formation in this kind of world have already placed severe strains on democratic practices. Either democratic forms will be placed under even greater pressure in the future, or we will need to find more effective methods of publicizing and judging proposals for social change.

Nondemocratic societies present an additional dilemma for modern man. The problem of a large part of the world is how revolutions may be fought against dictatorial governments that are buttressed by all the devices available to them in our scientifically sophisticated days. The technology of totalitarianism now includes weapons so powerful as seemingly to eliminate the possibility of opposition. Karl Mannheim pointed out, "Barricades, the symbols of revolution, are relics of an age when they were built up against cavalry."[2] Add to refined armament for repression new organizational possibilities for centralized administration, thorough saturation through a monopoly of improved mass media, and psychological refinements of brainwashing and terror. All this suggests that the road to freedom is now a dismal and perhaps impossible trail—unless we can make new discoveries in means for expressing the aspirations of men toward liberty.

In addition to such sociological factors, there are powerful theological and ethical considerations impelling us to a renewed search for more adequate methods. The Christian view of God yokes power to righteousness. These two attributes are held together in unity. In a basic harmony of ends and means, God's purposes are good and he has strength to accomplish them. Righteousness is seen as contributing to strength. The love of God is a gentle persuader and yet carries unparalleled power. Finite man has not understood the sources of greatest power because he has diluted the radical ranges of the love of God as seen in Christ.

In one form or another Christian theology carries a doctrine of enabling grace. No matter what restrictions may be placed on man by the limitations of his nature, God releases new possibilities in those who turn to him. Righteousness and power can also be expressed through men. We ought never to become so cynical as to say that love is unrelated to strength. Christians are constantly called upon to keep their means as well as their ends under review.

Some of our most troublesome challenges to conscience fall in this area. Vexatious problems arise partly because of the resistances of imperfect social situations. Evil choices made by others always limit what can be done. Hemmed in by such restrictions, how can we combat evil without acting like the devil? How can we enlarge the range of good so long as we are not living in a society of angels? We continuously approximate rather than attain the perfect expression of righteousness and love. Thoughtful Christians always remain uncomfortable about the compromises they feel they must make in the area of techniques and strategies.

Especially is this so since we know there must be a vast range of possibilities that we have never seriously attempted to understand. Even in quite limited circumstances there are methods available of which we are not aware. For one thing, these hidden alternatives must surely include more refined uses of customary forms of persuasion and social decision. In addition, we are also quite properly haunted by the possibility of new orders of social power that we have never heretofore seriously considered. For example, even specialists within the Christian community have only explored around the edges of the Biblical suggestion that evil can be overcome with good. What are possible social implications of the fifty-third chapter of Isaiah? In what sense may the suffering of a man or a nation heal another? Except possibly within the family, even our most enlightened methods still fall considerably short of "Bless those who persecute you. . . . Repay no one evil for evil" (Rom. 12:14, 17). By various theological devices, we have commonly dismissed as utopian or irrelevant the suggestions of Jesus about turning the other cheek, giving the cloak, or going the second mile (Matt. 5:39–41). Yet it is right that we should never have felt entirely at ease with our explaining away these difficult

sayings. We are too easily prone to whatever compromises suit
our selfish interests, and our so-called explanations may prove
to be false rationalizations. Among the more profound dimensions of the Christian view of God are concepts concerning
salvation through a cross, resurrection after death, and victory
by way of defeat. Perhaps if we thought more profoundly about
the human situation, equally implausible certainties would
appear.

The practitioners of nonviolent resistance insist that they
are using methods which both approximate the norm of love
more closely and are socially more realistic. We ought at least
to investigate their claim. This is an intriguing case study in
the possibility of the "impossible" sayings of Jesus. Whatever
our final judgment may be, nonviolent direct action is a prom-
ising-enough method to merit exploration. At the moment, most
of us do not understand it well enough even to spell out its
procedures. We do not know what it is that ought to be examined. This is a greater lack than not choosing the best methods.
We are not even informed about the methods that might be
chosen.

More learned disputants have also fallen into confusion and
disagreement about nonviolent resistance because they have
not made it clear what they were talking about. That is, they
have not begun with a satisfactory definition of the subject. In
a way, this is understandable. A formal definition of nonviolent
resistance is difficult to construct because of the great variety of
techniques used by nonviolent resisters, presumably as part of
their general method. A first step toward meaningful analysis
and evaluation is to list these various techniques, and then to
isolate what is unique about campaigns of nonviolent resistance. For example, nonviolent campaigners (or Satyagrahis, in
Gandhi's terminology) use publicity. Yet not every act of distributing leaflets or issuing a press release is to be thought of
as an instance of nonviolent resistance. Resistance campaigns
have included strikes of workers, but not every industrial strike
ought to be labeled as nonviolent resistance. More conven-

tional actions of this sort, when used by resisters, are best thought of as supplementary to their unique program rather than as part of its distinctive character.

Among these supplementary techniques are negotiation, which Shridharani calls "the indispensable first step in the strategy of Satyagraha."[3] This is an attempt to build understanding, define issues, and if possible, reach agreement in direct bargaining. Throughout a campaign, as much use as possible is made of publicity and agitation, including literature, songs, slogan-shouting, speeches, meetings, mass media, parades, or demonstrations. At times an ultimatum may be issued, presenting selected demands with a time limit for compliance. Political action may be taken in elections, legislative bodies, or courts. Boycotts and strikes, with accompanying picketing, may be organized. Notable examples are the refusal of Indian resisters to buy British cloth, the Montgomery bus boycott, and a number of European instances of the general strike.

More clearly unique are the three methods of noncooperation, civil disobedience, and self-suffering. The first of these, noncooperation, extends to a broader front the withdrawal of services or support involved in the economic strike or boycott. Gandhi's noncooperation campaign was eventually to include surrender of honors and decorations received from the British government, withdrawal from legislative bodies and government service, and a boycott of schools. The Indian independence movement also began to set up substitute social forms. If this had been pressed far enough, it might have resulted in the appearance of a parallel government. As law courts were boycotted, some civil disputes were settled by private arbitration, or Congress Party schools were set up alongside British schools.

A second, more clearly distinctive aspect of nonviolent resistance is commonly referred to as "civil disobedience." Actually a better term would be "social disobedience," since more may be involved than violation of the regulations of political authority, as in breaking laws, infringing military or police instructions, or withholding taxes. Disobedience might also be undertaken against social custom or against economic or ecclesiastical authorities. Unlegislated social taboos may be violated or plant rules may be systematically disregarded. Recent illustrations are the sit-ins at lunch counters, stand-ins in ticket lines, live-ins in housing tracts, kneel-ins in churches, wade-ins at swimming pools and beaches. In each case the action performed has been forbidden by either law or custom. Or actions required by authorities may be refused, as in the long history of conscientious objectors to war.

Perhaps the most unique aspect of nonviolent resistance is the willing acceptance of whatever suffering follows nonconformity. Such consequent suffering may involve serious social ostracism, vigilante action, fines, imprisonment, and even death or martyrdom. It differs from criminal punishment both because no step is taken to hide the forbidden act or avoid the suffering, and because it comes as a result of conscientious objection to a law or regulation attacked on grounds of social justice rather than personal desire. The suffering of the resister is not necessarily courted, though sometimes it appears to be. The point is that it is not avoided. The resister acts with the expectation that a penalty is likely to follow. This is the action-suffering syndrome characterizing nonviolent resistance. It is suffering, however, taken upon oneself, rather than as in many other methods of social change, inflicted on one's opponents. In this sense it is the method of the cross rather than of the sword.

Nonviolent resistance may then be defined as open, peaceful, unconventional conduct considered socially desirable by the resister, and the willing endurance of the suffering that follows.[4] The nonconformity may consist either in performing an act forbidden by law or custom (social disobedience) or in refusing to perform a customary or required act (noncooperation). In either case the action is sufficiently unorthodox to release sanctions from a significant social group, a government body, or the general public.

Nonviolent resistance can be used by individuals in person-to-person situations. It has been suggested that one of its more frequent uses has been by women during the long historical period when culture defined wives as subjects of their husbands! Gandhi testified that he learned much about the method from his wife. It is also possible for isolated individuals by this method to protest against a practice of society as a whole. Whether or not their viewpoint is naïve in these days of mass society, both Gandhi and Thoreau had great confidence that social reform might be won through the civil disobedience of a very few select persons, or even of a single man. Here, however, we are concerned about nonviolent resistance as a social movement, used by groups against groups. It is here that both our chief problems and our more promising possibilities lie.

The definition formulated above does allow for considerable variation among resisters or campaigns. For example, forms of nonviolent resistance have sometimes been undertaken not so much as intentional strategy for bringing about a social change, as under the compulsion of personal witness by members of a group. A religious minority may continue their peculiar practices and accept the consequent persecution simply because they believe this to be right and not because of any conscious desire to extend the range of religious liberty. The social process involved is nevertheless one of nonviolent resistance. So long as man lives in society, personal witness has social effects. Nonconforming witness is an influence toward social change, whether it is so intended or not.

The method may be adopted by a group simply out of necessity, because it does not have the resources for violent action. This is often the case with colonial peoples. Or the method may be used as the expression of a deep commitment to a life philosophy of nonviolence. Or there may be a considerable mixture of these motivations. There is an important distinction involved here. Gandhi made a great deal of it, reserving the use of *Satyagraha* for action on principle, and assigning the term "passive resistance" to action undertaken as expediency. The first he considered to be the voluntary choice of spiritual strength, the second a decision forced by physical or material weakness.

Gandhi had a point in his insistence that, ideally, nonviolent resistance should be for participants an expression of a non-violent way of life. Without this, it would seem to be difficult to go very far toward maintaining the "open, peaceful" characteristics that are part of the definition of nonviolent resistance. As schooling for a campaign, participants might attend numerous ashrams or role-playing sessions. Yet if their non-violence remained purely expedient, it would more easily break down before increasing brutalities by the opposition. Gandhi was right in calling off his 1919 campaign when inner resources proved to be not yet great enough and violence erupted. Yet campaigns have been waged with rather minimal commitments to nonviolence as a way of life. In India, probably most participants simply saw this type of resistance as the only available alternative. For them, "nonviolence was a policy, and not a creed."[5] That Gandhi's total philosophy did not gain a large following is indicated by the ease with which an independent India adopted military defense as national policy. The distinction, therefore, between "passive resistance" and "Satyagraha" for practical purposes is not particularly meaningful. A mixture of motives is always present so long as participants are men and not gods. A wide range of "mixes" is possible under the heading "nonviolent resistance."

In addition to a discussion of the variety of activities to be included, it is also helpful to contrast nonviolent resistance with what is left out by definition. The pinkish blur that is the usual popular concept of nonviolent resistance can be more sharply focused by comparing this method with other kinds of nonviolent action.

In our culture there are four general methods used for attaining social goals without violence. These may be listed as: (1) publicity, including communication and education aimed at forming public opinion; (2) negotiation, or communication with smaller opposition groups, attempting to conclude a more formal and binding agreement, and including diplomacy as international negotiation; (3) democratic political action, such as elections, the passage of laws, and court decisions, procedures that are based on consent and do not activate the latent violence of the state; and (4) economic pressure, such as strikes, boycotts, or other expressions of economic power. Most of the activities classified under these headings cannot properly be called nonviolent resistance. Not every resignation of government officials in protest can be called noncooperation in a Gandhian sense. Making a liberal speech in a conservative community may lead to some suffering for the lecturer, but it is scarcely of such dimensions as to be nonviolent resistance.

Activities in any of these four areas may become nonviolent resistance when the group using them demonstrates the attitudes and convictions that characterize the nonviolent method (discussed in greater detail below) and when the action involved is sufficiently nonconforming to result in extraordinary suffering for the resisters. For example, demonstrations may be considered a form of nonviolent resistance when they are used in such size, in such places, in such forms, or for such purposes as to be unacceptable to established customs or law. It is quite socially acceptable to hold a Veterans Day parade with the blessing of the city fathers. It was a different matter under despotic conditions in Budapest on December 4, 1956, for marching women to bear flowers to the tomb of Hungary's Unknown Soldier, and there to sing their old national anthem and recite Petöfi's poem to freedom. The first strikes in the United States, insofar as they expressed the spirit of nonviolence, might well have approached nonviolent resistance. Now, however, this economic weapon is at least tolerated, whereas in many situations as novel a weapon as a general strike would be required to become an instance of nonviolent resistance.

Within any society some types of activity are approved and encouraged, or even required. Others are merely tolerated. Still other activities are forbidden and punished. They "are just not done" under given circumstances. This might be diagrammed in three concentric circles, moving from a central zone of approved behavior through an area of tolerated difference to an area of forbidden acts. Then the circles might be divided into four sectors, indicating the four groups of nonviolent means: publicity, negotiation, political action, economic pressure. As action in the spirit of nonviolence moves in any of the sectors into the zone of forbidden behavior, it tends to become nonviolent resistance.

To be sure, like social definitions in general, this involves a continuum, leaving borderline cases that are difficult to classify. It is also hard to define "murder" precisely, as a lengthy list of court cases would illustrate! Yet it is also clear that there is a category of nonviolent, resisting acts that has certain distinctive features and that has now become increasingly important as a subject for study.

Those who engage in nonviolent resistance have tended to emphasize certain characteristic personal attitudes and social policies. This complex of emphases, although by no means perfectly observed by its practitioners, nevertheless contributes a unique spirit or quality to the method. Some of the emphases contrast so significantly with our usual methods and thought processes that statements describing them seem paradoxical. The approach is considerably different from many other types of nonviolent methods, such as "Madison Avenue" publicity, "horse-trading" negotiation, or political action in "smoke-filled rooms."

For one thing, the nonviolent resister tends to stress willing the good for the person who does evil. On the negative side this means avoiding violence, or the direct use of physical force to destroy or damage life or property. Some exceptions have been made of property considered essentially harmful to society, as when Gandhi assented to the burning of British cloth. Typically, however, successful nonviolent resistance is victory without violence. It is also, on the positive side, a campaign for the best interests of opponents as well as of campaigners.

This attitude was dramatically expressed by Martin Luther King, Jr., in his talk from his front porch to the crowd that had gathered after the bombing of his home. "If you have weapons, take them home; if you do not have them, please do not seek to get them. We cannot solve this problem through retaliatory violence. We must meet violence with nonviolence. . . . We must love our white brothers, no matter what they do to us."[6]

Resisters tend to broaden the definition of violence far beyond its common meaning or precise, technical usage. Also to be rejected as violent are indirect destruction, personality injury, psychic terror, and violent thoughts. This is the spirit of the Sermon on the Mount: "You have heard that it was said to the men of old, 'You shall not kill; and whoever kills shall be liable to judgment.' But I say to you that every one who is angry with his brother shall be liable to judgment" (Matt. 5:21–22).

From his own religious tradition, Gandhi made Ahimsa (literally, "noninjury") the central article of his faith. He saw in the word a double meaning. "In its negative form, it means not injuring any living being whether by body or mind. . . . In its positive form, *Ahimsa* means the largest love, the greatest charity."[7] Gandhi insisted that a person should always treat an opponent as he would a member of his own family. A wrongdoer should be dealt with just as an erring father or son would be. "A Satyagrahi will always try to overcome evil by good, anger by love, untruth by truth, *himsa* by *ahimsa*."[8]

The resister tries, therefore, not to defeat an opponent, but to persuade him, not to humiliate him, but to contribute to his growth. A distinction is to be made between individuals and the system under which they work. An attack on evil is not to include an attack on persons who are doing evil. Instead, every effort is to be made to build understanding and avenues of cooperation. The vicious circle of hate is to be terminated by the counter expression of love.

A second emphasis of nonviolent resistance is on exerting social pressure by moral action. The righteous man can never acquiesce in evil. His whole life is to become a testimony against wrong. Gandhi wrote in *Young India*, "I know too that

I shall never know God if I do not wrestle with and against evil even at the cost of life itself."[9] His method might be called nonviolent insistence. It is aggressive instead of passive. Nonviolent resistance consists not in suffering accidental atrocity, even in the serious form in which it was met by Jews under Hitler, because of an ancestry for which they were not responsible. Nonviolent resistance involves positive, purposive action. The initiative is typically in the hands of the resisters. By conduct that disrupts existing arrangements, they carry the struggle to the opposition. Their strategy is not defense but attack, not a single battle but a continuing campaign.

Such nonviolent direct action is far from nonresistance, even though the two are often confused. Nonresistance is not necessarily submission to one's opponent or compliance with evil commands. It is rather the endurance of injustice without overt protest. It is to this extent removal from the conflict and going about one's business as though nothing were happening. In a highly interdependent society, of course, complete abstinence from controversy and absolute nonresistance are impossible. Even going about one's business, and avoiding certain other acts considered wrong, exerts a social influence— though that particular kind of influence may be only partially praiseworthy. Everyone, short of Robinson Crusoe on an island, inevitably engages in some form of social propaganda by private action.

Nonviolent resistance goes well beyond this minimal impact, however, to a full-throated proclamation. Intense moral passion is likely to be expressed in vigorous and robust conduct. Especially to those whose interests are challenged, nonviolent resistance may give the impression of uncivil, turbulent behavior by unreasonable fanatics. Sometimes the denunciations of resisters have been so fierce as to forget to distinguish sin from sinner. Although the following quotation is not typical of all campaigns, it does help to balance the too frequent representation of nonviolent resisters as spiritless, hesitant, or cowardly. Otherwise gentle Quakers, facing the intolerance of Massachusetts

Puritanism, repeatedly erupted with such expletives as: "As for ye, ye men of New-England, . . . ye shame of men, ye refuse of mankind; higher than the highest in profession of godliness, lower than the lowest in the power thereof. . . . Ye serpents, ye generation of vipers."[10] Of course, those were days of a less refined vocabulary for controversy. Vividness of phrase and intensity of intolerance were common. Puritans at the same time were referring to Quakers as "Satan's hirelings" and "ravening wolves." The colonial governor is reported to have shouted at a Quaker witness in court, "Hold your tongue, you prating housewife; you are led by the spirit of the devil to run about the country a wandering, like whores and rogues."[11]

Those woman suffragists who picketed the White House and went to jail were also zealously insistent on their rights. They clung to their banners when police tried to confiscate them or they started another "watch fire" after one had been put out. They argued with the judge, or later refused to speak, stand, or recognize the court in any way. They refused to pledge good behavior or to pay fines. When lodged in jail, they demanded treatment as political prisoners. There is little wonder that they were called "daughters of obsession."[12]

Social reform movements are typically divided into militant and moderate wings. Nonviolent resisters are normally to be classified among the militants. Theirs is a deep sense of mission to which they subordinate other life interests. They are engaged in trying to accelerate progress to its maximum tempo. Theirs is the motto on the signs of contemporary Negro demonstrations: Now!

At basic points where vital interests are involved, social change is never possible without severe conflict. Nonviolent resisters have been realistic about this. In their campaigns they have not hesitated to initiate controversy or to advance into the sharpest confrontation of forces.

Not only does nonviolent resistance reject violence on the one hand and avoid nonresistance on the other. It is also marked by its emphasis on truth as force. At its best, neither falsehood nor concealment has a place in the method. Because of the secrecy involved in the underground railroad for American slaves and in the resistance movement that smuggled Jews out of Hitler's reach, these cannot, strictly speaking, be classified as nonviolent resistance.

Gandhi in particular developed the theory of Satyagraha, or "truth force." He insisted that reliance on truth brought strength to the resister, since honesty and integrity are essentials of the pure life. It also strengthens the appeal of the movement to others. They know that when the Satyagrahi speaks he has no mental reservations. The hearer therefore knows that his words are to be taken literally and not as a propaganda statement or bargaining position. Furthermore, there is a power about truth to commend itself over the long run to the rational capacities of men. This claim of Gandhi's will need to be tested in later analysis.

Reliance on truth nurtures an attitude of humility. Gandhi recognized that finite minds cannot claim to know truth in the absolute sense. Since every man is a seeker, no man should destroy those who differ with him. Rather, he should be willing open-mindedly to learn from his opponent and to modify his own demands accordingly. Gandhi emphasized this when Muriel Lester was returning to England to lecture on the Indian situation. Gandhi advised her to discuss her findings with the viceroy, since he might be able to disprove some of her conclusions.[13]

At the same time that Gandhi tried to hold an open mind, he also exhibited deep conviction. He spoke positively, emphatically, and persistently. His opponents must often have wondered what modification he had made in deference to truth in their position! The nonviolent resister is not alone in this dilemma. Every sensitive person is pulled between the desire to be true to convictions he now holds and at the same time to be open to improved convictions for the future. The nonviolent resister tries to take both claims seriously.

Devotion to truth characteristically has been reflected in the general practice of openly announcing plans in advance for campaigns of nonviolent resistance—though not necessarily in such detail as to allow opponents to nip a demonstration in the bud. The "freedom riders" on Southern buses in the United States gave prior notification even though this allowed the mobs to gather. Again and again those who practiced civil disobedience informed the police when and where they expected to break the law. Gandhi pointed out that this policy solved the problem of preventing espionage within his own movement. Where nothing was concealed, no spies were necessary!

Gandhi went to great lengths to preserve this kind of rectitude. In distributing prohibited literature, he advised, "Satyagrahis should as far as possible write their names and addresses as sellers so that they may be traced easily when wanted by the Government for prosecution."[14] When an official agreed to withdraw an insulting or demanding letter, Gandhi insisted that no copy be made before the letter was returned. That would make the withdrawal untruth. In his movement there was no place for such cunning.

Another descriptive paradox is found in the emphasis of nonviolent resistance on social reform through self-purification. One's opponents are to be changed partly by changing oneself.

This involves acceptance of some responsibility for social wrongs because of one's own unrighteousness. If one does not admit his own mistakes, he is persisting in untruth. This barters genuine strength for a false sense of prestige. The resister is asked not only to denounce evil deeds in others but also to repent himself. He is to cultivate both alertness to social wrongs and thoroughness in recognizing personal imperfections. Parallel to the words of Jesus about the speck and the log in the eye (Matt. 7:3–5) is Gandhi's statement: "I have always held that it is only when one sees one's own mistakes with a convex lens and does just the reverse in the case of others, that one is able to arrive at a just estimate of the two."[15] Characteristically, he wrote, "When therefore untruth was discovered in the Ashram, I readily pleaded guilty for it myself."[16] When incidents of violence led him to terminate his 1919 campaign, he referred to this as his "Himalayan blunder" and said: "I must undergo personal cleansing. . . . I am in the unhappy position of a surgeon proved skill-less to deal with an admittedly dangerous case. I must either abdicate or acquire greater skill."[17]

Part of the significance of Gandhi's fasts was to contribute to personal spiritual cleansing. The effects of fasts on others will be discussed later. After one fast he wrote: "The fast was an uninterrupted twenty-one days' prayer whose effect I can feel even now. . . . All fasting, if it is a spiritual act, is an intense prayer or a preparation for it. It is a yearning of the soul to merge in the divine essence."[18] A fast is a denial of self, which is an indispensable condition for spiritual growth. "In the end . . . ," said Gandhi, "there is only one basis for the whole idea of fasting, and that is purification."[19]

Emphasis on personal change has characteristically led toward the cultivation of a total pattern of life among resisters. Group expectations fortified approved qualities and practices, especially in the inner circle or leadership group. Statements listing appropriate attitudes and conduct played a similar part in campaigns in British India and in the American South. Training sessions and worship services have been designed to contribute to such personal development. Gandhi himself pushed the nonviolent life to the radical extreme of vegetarianism, continence, and nonpossession. Though few followers went that far, individuals and groups did take vows of extensive self-denial.

The citizens of India as a whole were challenged to extensive domestic reform. In addition to his campaigns for independence, Gandhi always placed great emphasis on his "constructive program" of social welfare measures to be undertaken by the Indian people themselves. Gandhi held that the correction of wrongs within India was a necessary prerequisite to gaining concessions from Great Britain. For him the doing of justice must precede the gaining of justice. So long, for example, as untouchability remained, he felt it right that India should remain in bondage. At one point when the drive for independence seemed to be gaining concessions, he suspended it to concentrate on untouchability. He expected change first in his own people, and then among the English. "Swaraj [independence]," said he, "does not consist in the change of Government; that would be merely the form. The substance that I am hankering after is a real change of heart on the part of the people."[20]

A last major emphasis of nonviolent resistance is on accepting rather than inflicting suffering. The extraordinary aim is conquest through suffering. This is a process of winning battles by the spilling of one's own blood. Victory is expected not by way of more powerful retaliation but by more persistent sacrifices. All this is regarded not as a "weapon of the weak" but as an expression of the strong.

Gandhi calls Satyagraha "the law of suffering." He maintained, "Nothing can shake me from the conviction that, given a good cause, suffering for it advances it as nothing else has done."[21] In similar vein, when the Washington courts began to give their longest prison sentences to the militant suffragists, their leader, Alice Paul, said: "The Administration has fired its heaviest gun. From now on we shall win and they will lose."[22]

If anything, resisters have shown some tendency to increase their own physical losses, not only by pushing toward more extreme conduct, but also by assuming some liability for the needs of their opponents. Resisters have not always come up to their professed ideals at this point. Yet at their best, they have been ready to return good for evil even when that was a costly policy. Gandhi several times refused to take advantage of the government when it was hard pressed by other circumstances. In South Africa at the time of the Boer War and of the Zulu rebellion, Gandhi called off his movement and organized an ambulance corps to aid the government. When the plague broke out among the Negroes near Johannesburg, Gandhi organized medical help. In India, resisters gave food and blankets to the police, as the police stayed on duty to stop a demonstration. In his instructions to Satyagrahis in India, Gandhi stressed their duty to protect officials from insult or assault even at the risk of life.

There is much about this ancient yet neglected method which recalls the words of the apostle Paul: "As servants of God we commend ourselves in every way: through great endurance, in afflictions, hardships, calamities, beatings, imprisonments, tumults, labors, watching, hunger; by purity, knowledge, forbearance, kindness, the Holy Spirit, genuine love, truthful speech, and the power of God; with the weapons of righteousness for the right hand and for the left; in honor and dishonor, in ill repute and good repute. We are treated as impostors, and yet are true; as unknown, and yet well known; as dying, and behold we live; as punished, and yet not killed; as sorrowful, yet always rejoicing; as poor, yet making many rich; as having nothing, and yet possessing everything" (II Cor. 6:4–10).

The more common training manuals for modern conflict would revise this considerably. In our nuclear, affluent, status-striving times, the descriptive text might better speak of our coming to have everything in military power, only to find that we possess nothing for security; our having banished hardship, and yet being tormented by existential anxiety; our being exceedingly well introduced publicity-wise, only to remain alienated strangers; our being incomparably rich, yet making many poor. Such contrasts between existing reality and accepted ideal add urgency to our next inquiry. How does nonviolent resistance work out in actual practice?

2

DIVISION AND CONFLICT IN THE RESISTANCE PROCESS

When Gandhi left South Africa, General Smuts remarked, "The saint has left our shores, I sincerely hope for ever." This should not be a surprising combination of sentiments. The recognition of sainthood, which Smuts genuinely attributed to Gandhi, is easily followed by a desire to keep one's distance. Rejection and attraction are often part of the same reaction. While we beckon with one hand, we wave off with the other.

Men did this often enough with Jesus. One of the earliest instances was described in language paralleling the Smuts quotation. After the healing of the Gadarene demoniac, the villagers came out to see the wonder-worker, but their words expressed their fear rather than their awe. "Behold, all the city came out to meet Jesus; and when they saw him, they begged him to leave their neighborhood." (Matt. 8:34.)

A similar ambivalence infects the study of nonviolent resistance. The student's first exposure is likely to arouse both antipathy and appreciation within him. Most persons initially react on the basis of long-established predispositions, accepting or rejecting the method uncritically without the painstaking analysis necessary to work through initial ambivalence and hasty reaction to a more mature judgment. Careful research is essential to adequate evaluation. It will not do to settle for wishful thinking, confusing one's hopes and daydreams with reality. Nor is partial observation enough, relying on one or two examples to establish generalizations. This is too much like the blind men judging the elephant by only a leg or a tail.

An important aspect of a more scholarly approach is a comparison of various campaigns, searching for typical progressions or patterns of social interaction. Such an examination of historical data illuminates the psychosocial dynamics involved. Yet this life-cycle approach should not suggest any inevitability of responses or identity in situations. Some stages may be greatly abbreviated or even missing in some campaigns. Peculiar circumstances modify the sequence of occurrences. The practical rub-a-dub of agitation, the turmoil on the city streets, does not fit neatly into detailed molds prepared in a professor's study. Yet general similarities do emerge. The concept of a natural history of social movements allows for the fact that each campaign is significantly different, at the same time that a similar underlying process may characteristically reappear. There are tendencies or probabilities in social responses. A knowledge of these provides a superior basis for planning by those who wish to influence persons in society, and also provides a foundation of understanding for ethical evaluation that is realistically oriented.

Incorporated in the following findings are careful studies of Gandhi's campaigns, the struggle for religious liberty of Quakers in the Massachusetts Bay Colony, the militant wing of the woman suffrage movement in the United States, American conscientious objectors to World War I, the resistance to the Nazis in Denmark, and insofar as materials are now available, the civil rights campaigns among Negroes in the contemporary South. Less thorough coverage of numerous other instances has also helped to confirm the conclusion that there is a typical general process of nonviolent resistance.

Three groups are involved in interaction: (1) the resisters themselves, those who are actively engaged in nonconformity related to social change; (2) their opponents, who are engaged in contrary action in opposition to the resisters; and (3) spectators or third parties, those who are not directly engaged in the dispute, but who are sufficiently involved to be aware of events and who may come to throw their support to one side or the other. The latter group of those who are initially by-standers includes both those in the immediate society (community or nation) in which the dispute is taking place and also those at a greater distance, as in other nations.

The lines of interaction among these three groups can be seen as falling into three typical periods. These are not sharply divided chronologically. There is likely to be considerable overlapping. Furthermore, unsuccessful campaigns do not run through all three stages. Yet these periods are sufficiently typical and helpful to understanding that we may use them as a logical convenience. The three stages include: (1) a period of intensification of conflict, marked by the initiative of the re-sisters, the reaction of opponents, and deepening controversy; (2) a realignment of forces in which the spectators or third parties also play a large part; and (3) a period of reform and reconciliation, involving readjustment and accommodation to new patterns of power, and developing understandings between former antagonists.

The nonviolent resistance portion of any social agitation is initiated as the conduct of resisters begins to be sufficiently un-conventional to call for social punishment. It is helpful here to pick up again the concentric circle representation introduced in the first chapter. There it was suggested that an inner circle might represent activities approved and encouraged in a particular culture. The next concentric circle would bound an area of action that is customarily disapproved and yet tolerated. A third circle would represent acts so seriously deviant as to be forbidden and punished. It is here that the action of nonviolent resisters lies.

It is useful now to introduce a fourth circle to indicate an area of utterly proscribed action. Conduct in this area is regarded as so serious a threat by a society as a whole that it will be fanatically and rather unanimously opposed even to the point of complete liquidation of those who attempt it. An example might be Jewishness within the Nazi Party, which would be dealt with differently than, let us say, religious worship in the general population. Or, in some cultural situations, racial intermarriage is proscribed behavior, whereas integrated public school attendance is only punished behavior.

If he is to provide his unique contribution to social progress, the nonviolent resister must cross the threshold of untolerated behavior. Until he does that he is merely using customary methods of publicity, negotiation, or political or economic action. Whatever additional stimulus is provided by nonviolent resistance begins as socially unacceptable behavior is undertaken. Ordinarily, at any rate, the resister will also need to stop short of the area of proscribed behavior. If he goes beyond that point, he is likely to trigger an overwhelmingly negative response. Opponents then can be expected completely to close their minds, solidify their previous position, and move to wipe out the innovating group. If nonconformity goes too far, then opponents and bystanders feel that there is justification for sternly repressive violence. Part of the task of the nonviolent resister is to remove this justification. Action in the proscribed area could still be classified as nonviolent resistance. Usually, however, it would appear to be an unwise use of the method, one which, under given social circumstances, is doomed to defeat.

Leaders of nonviolent movements, of course, may not know in which area a particular act will prove to lie until they have tried it. The conduct might be too novel to have been attempted before. Besides, societies do not publish lists of all possible actions with the degrees of intensity of opposition that will be applied. Insofar as practical considerations of strategy are taken seriously, occasional probing operations and continuous adaptability are called for. Part of the greatness of Gandhi lay in the fact that he was quite aware of this.

The area of toleration, in which deviation is accepted without punishment, tends to be broader in open or dynamic societies than in closed or static situations. A democratic society, with plural centers of power, is in general more permissive than a tightly controlled dictatorship. A society that is accustomed to change or that is committed to improvement as an important social goal is likely to deal more kindly with its minorities, since minorities are seen to be the seedbed of progress. A greater amount of apparently eccentric or even dangerous behavior will be tolerated in order not to impede criticisms that may turn out to be helpful. Furthermore, wider deviation may be allowed with respect to some areas of activity than to others. A common illustration is the greater freedom given to technological invention than is allowed to social innovation. Any field in which powerful vital interests are involved does not offer as much latitude for maneuver by the social critic.

The scope of the zone of tolerated difference also varies from time to time. It may be contracted in times of emergency such as war. A nonviolent resister reaches the boundaries of forbidden and of proscribed behavior sooner when a population feels insecure or fearful. A nation that is facing military defeat is likely to deal more severely with its conscientious objectors to war. A similar effect may be produced by a change in government or a shift in strategy by opponents of the resisters. Or more serious penalties may be imposed when a movement that has previously had only nuisance value comes to have a serious chance for success. It is not surprising that the current movement for equality of racial opportunity should be marked by severe conflict. We stand on the edge of such great changes here that defenders of the *status quo* bring up their biggest guns for a last-ditch stand.

In any of these various ways the process of nonviolent resistance may be initiated because conduct previously tolerated has come to be punished or proscribed. The typical sequence of nonconformity followed by punishment may also begin, however, because reformers have become more deviant in their behavior. Demonstrators protesting against nuclear weapons in London in September, 1961, were arrested not when they stood in Trafalgar Square listening to speeches or chanting, "Ban the bomb!" but when they sat down in the streets and could be charged with obstructing traffic. In the United States, religious conscientious objectors have met punishment by government as they took a more absolutist stand, such as refusing to accept the noncombatant or alternative services provided by law.

Resisters have often, though not always, undertaken more radical forms of expression as a campaign lengthened. The noncooperation movement led by Gandhi in 1920–1922 was to move through stages from minor to major withdrawals from government activities. The Indian salt satyagraha moved from Gandhi's march to the sea to "raids" on the salt depots and disobedience of other repressive laws. Woman suffragists picketed the White House, first with milder and then with more militant banners. This was followed with "watch fires" to be kept perpetually burning near the White House. Finally President Wilson was burned in effigy. All these were attempts to develop procedures to meet specific and changing situations. When resistance to change has not been overcome by their first approaches, reformers have frequently sought what the suffragists called an "accelerating tactic."

Deviant actions by resisters either may include novel methods of publicity to win support for an eventual change (as propaganda by processions), or they may involve the immediate practice of the end sought (as worshiping according to the rite forbidden by an intolerant government, or an interracial group swimming at a previously segregated beach). In either case this insistence on doing what the resisters regard as right poses a serious dilemma for their opponents. If they allow an effective method of publicity, it is only a question of time until they lose to the resisters. If they allow the continued practice of the end, they have already lost. In both cases the opponents must either surrender or punish. Facing these alternatives, they are likely to invoke social or legal sanctions—though in a more complicated reaction pattern than is often portrayed.

The initial reaction of opponents is often one of confusion and indecision. Police faced by the early Gandhian demonstrations or store managers who experienced the first sit-ins at their lunch counters did not know what to do. These were actions contrary to all previous experience. The unexpected confrontation did not fit their definition of the social situation. Established policies and habit patterns provided no ready answer.

They were thrown off balance and often had to improvise some sort of gesture to save the situation. As in any pressure for social change, the basic issue for defenders of the *status quo* is concession or coercion. To what extent shall demands be partially met in order to ease the attack, purchasing silence with a sop? Or to what extent shall available power be mobilized to continue the conflict? In other words, what is the most effective strategy for defense? Throughout a struggle it is the answers to these questions that define the policy of opponents.

Any force that is used can be either legal or extralegal. It can be exerted either by government or by other community groups. Or the two may be combined, as when mobs are allowed essentially to become instruments of government policy. When during the sit-ins and the freedom rides, police either stood aside or arrived late, mobs to this extent were tolerated and allowed to take the law into their own hands.

It was the general public that applied the sanction of social ostracism to conscientious objectors. Newspaper editorials fanned the flames with words like, "There is no type of criminal so repulsive to the patriotic citizen as the cringing, skulking coward who refuses to fight for his flag and country."[1] Clergymen referred to pacifists in World War I collectively as "a bunch of cranks" or individually as "a man who uses his religion to cloak a yellow streak."[2]

In other extralegal actions, crowds of segregationists have tried to prevent racial integration by intimidation or violence. Counterdemonstrators have raced through the streets with placards and Confederate flags, shouting insults at Negroes. Rocks have been thrown and bombs exploded. Verbal abuse and threats have been interjected in continuous series of telephone calls. Children have been expelled from school and parents discharged from jobs. Those sitting-in at lunch counters have had food dumped on their heads and lighted cigarettes crushed on their bodies. Mobs have gathered at school entrances, and pickets have informed the public that GOD IS THE AUTHOR OF SEGREGATION or THE MAYOR IS A RAT. One woman who walked into school through a jeering crowd said: "I have never had people look at me like that in my life, I mean with hate, like they wanted to kill me. . . . That was a long walk."[3]

The variety of possible responses by opponents is considerably greater than this, however. Whether it is action by public authorities or by private groups, a more sophisticated choice may be made of tactics expected to be even more effective. It is possible, though rare, to try to overcome resistance with kindness. President Wilson first tried to nullify the influence of the suffragist pickets by his own courtesy. On one cold day he had them invited into the East Room of the White House to warm up—although the suffragists did not accept this offer of aid from the opposition camp. In South Africa, money found on resisters was applied toward fines, even when those sentenced had rejected the option of a fine. This helped to empty the jails as fast as the demonstrators flooded them. A cat-and-mouse policy has been rather common, alternating periods of severity and mildness. Such a hot and cold policy may be designed to weaken the morale of resisters by imposing maximum inconvenience and uncertainty, while at the same time incurring the minimum chance of making martyrs and of arousing public opposition. Selective sanctions may be applied, as in arresting only part of the demonstrators. Or preventive sanctions have been used, culling out leaders to forestall demonstrations.

Opponents may try to incite violence among the resisters, knowing that the public will then support more severe repressive measures. By their own needling response, opponents may directly try to provoke retaliation, or they may introduce *agents provocateurs* among the resisters. Opponents may also try to divide and conquer by offering rewards to part of the protesting group, or by minor concessions designed to split the moderate from the radical reformers, or by spreading rumors of dissension or defections from the movement. Martin Luther King, Jr., in his account of the Montgomery bus boycott recounts some of these efforts, including the rumor that Negro leaders were buying big cars while their followers walked, or the attempt to encourage other leaders to take over the protest.[4]

Frequently the opposition seems initially to misinterpret the seriousness of the situation, thinking nonviolence to be an indication of weakness and underestimating the amount of potential support. Often it is assumed that minimal coercion will repress the trouble. Then when the protest continues, or when the resisters gain even larger numbers or engage in even more unacceptable acts, an increased threat must be dealt with.

In general, the reaction of the opposition is increased severity of punishment. Having committed themselves to the method of punitive power, and finding the first penalties inadequate, they tend to add more of the same. Given a persistent and aggressive resistance group, it is almost inevitable that this should be the characteristic reaction of their opponents.

The first reaction of authorities was mild when suffragists picketed the White House. They were not officially interfered with for almost six months. Wilson was not only courteous but also opposed to creating martyrs by arrests. As their banners became more irritating, the police, instead of protecting the pickets from the crowds, for a short time allowed rowdies to tear down the offensive signs. Then police began to arrest pickets, but the first ones arrested were never brought to trial. After several days of this, groups were sentenced to three days' imprisonment or a twenty-five-dollar fine. Then a group sentenced to sixty days was pardoned after two days. After a brief respite, sentences began to build up again until they reached six and seven months.

During the salt satyagraha in India, the British moved from single to mass arrests to more repressive laws, including suppression of publicity and assembly. When most of the teachers of Norway refused to join the Nazi teachers organization, the Quisling government first threatened loss of jobs, then began arrests, and finally transported a group to brutal treatment in a labor camp in the extreme north.[5]

One of the most dramatic illustrations is the reaction of Puritan leadership in the Massachusetts Bay Colony to the arrival of Quakers. The first to come were immediately imprisoned and deported. As others continued to come, whipping was added to imprisonment and deportation, and then ear-cropping. When all this proved to be ineffective, Quakers were banished on pain of death. Finally, from 1659 to 1661, four Quakers were hanged, including one woman.

Conflict is even sharper and the chances for resolution even less when both resisters and their opponents are highly motivated. Not only are rather obvious group interests involved, but these are often reinforced on both sides by idealistic or religious convictions. Both the reformers and those who protect the existing situation are convinced of the righteousness of their cause. The Puritans, guided by their clergy, were sure they were defending God's way. The British may have been imperialists, but they saw themselves also as benefactors of India. There are conscientious persecutors as well as conscientious objectors. As one Southern governor is quoted as saying about those sitting-in at lunch counters, "They think they can violate any law, especially if they have a Bible in their hands; our law enforcement officers have their Bibles too."[6]

Under such circumstances neither side is prepared to give up easily. Important group interests are at stake. Considerable private investment of emotional capital has been made and must be defended. A public position has been taken from which it is not easy to back down. Ultimate religious concerns may seem threatened. On any important issue, a struggle involving nonviolent resistance is no less a desperate encounter than major conflicts using other methods. The outcome is, however, determined on different grounds. The central consideration is not the amount of armament that can be deployed, as in war, or the economic endurance of the two sides, as in a strike. It is, rather, a contest basically between the persistence of the resisters under suffering and the ability of opponents to increase the severity of penalties.

In successful campaigns the resisters muster enough resources of persistence and courage to continue or even expand their nonconformity into new demands and less tolerable acts. During such intensification of conflict, occasional resisters may be responding neurotically and compulsively. Most participants, however, seem to have found, through inner discipline and group support, an endurance that has often risen to heroic courage.

In spite of harsh penalties the number of Quakers coming to colonial Massachusetts constantly increased. Two days after Mary Fisher and Ann Austin had been deported, eight other Quakers sailed into Boston harbor. In spite of increasing severity, the same persons came back again and again "to look the bloody laws in the face." Although about sixty years of age, Elizabeth Hooton came to Boston at least six times, being expelled each time, and was four times whipped through several towns out of the jurisdiction.[7] Even the death penalty proved to be no deterrent. While William Leddra was being tried for his life, Wenlock Christison, who had already been banished upon pain of death, walked calmly into the courtroom.[8] Then while Christison was on trial, Edward Wharton, who had also been ordered to leave the colony or forfeit his life, wrote from his home in Salem that he was still there.[9] Such a succession of applications for execution identified a people who were not to be turned aside by any terrors their persecutors might devise.

Again and again the followers of Gandhi stood steady in spite of *lathi* blows or even occasional gunfire. Gandhi correctly stated, "It cannot be too often repeated that we court imprisonment."[10] Like others who have more recently followed the same instruction, no resistance was to be offered to arrest, and imprisonment was to be chosen rather than paying a fine.[11]

When the woman suffrage pickets were warned that they would be arrested, they nevertheless continued picketing. Women repeatedly went back on the picket line after they were released from jail, the same incorrigibles being arrested again and again. Julia Emory was reported to have been arrested thirty-four times.[12] After the most severe sentences of the campaign had been imposed, there appeared the longest picket line yet arrested.[13] When the sentences were suspended two days later, most of these again returned to picket the White House and were once more arrested.[14] Released pending their court appearances, they picketed for the third time and were again arrested.[15] This group of perpetual picketers received sentences ranging from six days to six months—and almost all of them went on a hunger strike when imprisoned.

Not all resisters are able to live up to such standards. Some drop out of the ranks when heavier opposition appears. Every reform movement includes those who are ready to engage in the more conventional forms of protest, such as signing petitions or making modest contributions, but who are prone to disappear when social pressure becomes greater. Not all those arrested come back for another jail experience. Some of the Massachusetts Quakers withdrew in the face of suffering. A few of those in Salem moved on to settle in Rhode Island or on Nantucket. William Robinson lamented the fact that six Quakers banished on pain of death had not returned and had thus "fled the cross, and . . . given the enemy cause to triumph."[16] In India some fled before the *lathi* charges of the police. The militancy of some conscientious objectors lessened as pressures increased.

Increasing severity of punishment has a double effect on resisters. It weeds out the weak, but at the same time it increases the determination of the strong. Attacks may lower the morale of some. At the same time they raise the morale of others. Resisters may be convinced that an opponent's violence betrays his weakness, and that suffering is to be welcomed because it will bring victory. For some, brutality stiffens resolution and increases zeal. When opponents resort to violence they make it less likely that their persuasive efforts will succeed. Any verbal utterance is interpreted in the framework of accompanying acts. The severity of the Puritans made the Quakers all the more certain that the Puritans were anti-Christ. The repressive measures of the British etched more deeply their imperialist image in India.

Formerly passive onlookers may also begin to view the situation in a light more favorable to the resisters. After the freedom riders had met mob violence, other riders decided to join the group and began converging on Alabama and Mississippi. Even in the early days of a campaign the severe persecution designed to eliminate the resisting group may actually somewhat increase its size. A certain number of new recruits is attracted from those sufficiently predisposed to be moved by what appears to them to be deepening injustice.

The experience of repression may also lead resisters to step up their demands, which again is the precise opposite of the outcome intended by their opponents' tactics. It is also true that during this stage of the campaign the demands of the resisters may be reduced, particularly when this seems necessary to make constructive agreements possible. In other cases convictions are so intensified as to raise the asking price. A number of conscientious objectors during World War II, having accepted alternate service camps, were moved by their experience there to demand complete freedom from conscription. The Montgomery bus boycott did not originally challenge segregated seating as such. When the leaders, however, saw so little response to appeals to reason and felt the full sting of deep hostility, they filed a court suit challenging bus segregation as such.

Punishment also increases determination as those persecuted draw together into a more closely knit fellowship. Facing hostility, they tend to associate only with their own kind. This increases their impenetrability to contrary influences. As group morale develops, individuals are less likely to defect and more likely to persist. When their own group association comes to mean so much more to them, they are more likely to act according to group standards of courageous resistance. They are then even more reluctant to lose the group approval that they have come so deeply to treasure.

Consciously or unconsciously resisters use a variety of methods of social control to generate cause consciousness and group support. Songs, slogans, and symbols play an important part. The *khaddar*, or homespun, worn by the Satyagrahis, became a tie between the like-minded. Paper clips worn in lapels for a time reminded the Nazi-dominated Norwegians to "keep together." In the American racial protest the strains of "We Shall Overcome" have held many a demonstrator steady in the face of danger. Agitation, education, and common experiences provide a characteristic group definition of the situation and of the acceptable reaction to it.

The early Christians formed such a closely knit group standing together in opposition to the larger social environment. During periods of persecution, those being examined by the authorities were not left to stand alone. At every opportunity they were surrounded by fellow believers, whose presence emphasized the group standard and lent a resolution born of vital fellowship in common faith. The supporting group was strongly felt to include also a host of heavenly witnesses—God, Christ, and the martyrs who had gone before. Such a sense of solidarity at last affected a number of Christians who had decided to make the offering demanded by the state. Still their fellows labored with them until, as the faithful reported, "we actually called back some who were even mounting to the Capitol to obey the summons to sacrifice."[17] Other Christians presented themselves for punishment so readily that their eagerness to die was regarded by officials as hardly short of suicide.

Massachusetts Quakers developed a close unity of Christian affection. Daniel Gould's narrative preserves a firsthand account of the fellowship among those in prison on the day Robinson and Stephenson were executed. He describes it as

a time of love. . . . And many sweet and heavenly sayings they gave unto us, being themselves filled with comfort. . . . While we were embracing each other, and taking leave, with full and tender hearts (God knows) the officers, and men appointed (like Friends butchers) came in, and took the two from us, as sheep for the slaughter, and had them away to the execution, where they were hanged to death.[18]

There is a strikingly similar contemporary testimony to the deep comradeship possible in voluntary imprisonment. One account of the civil rights campaign in Albany, Georgia, says, "The experience of jail itself—sometimes with sixteen or more persons in a cell made for four—helped many persons to experience the sense of a joyful, suffering *Koinonia* that they had never known in any church."[19]

During the independence movement, it became almost a disgrace for a patriotic Indian to remain out of jail. The first Bardoli landholders to be notified that they would be evicted if they did not pay taxes were congratulated by their friends. At the Washington woman suffrage headquarters, those released from jail were enthusiastically received and frequent dinners given in their honor. At one such banquet the toastmistress remarked, "Sixty days of jail is sixty days of honor."[20]

During the Greensboro, North Carolina, demonstrations, one college professor is reported to have said, "My entire class is in jail, so I might as well join them to give them their final examinations." In the February mass arrests of Negro leadership in Montgomery, Alabama, many voluntarily contacted the sheriff's office to see whether their names were on the list, and some were even disappointed when they were not. Speaking of the sit-inners, Mordecai Johnson, president of Howard University, told a Washington audience, "If your son becomes one, get on your knees and thank God."

These are pictures of groups who reverse the long-standing judgment that only criminals and undesirables go to jail. Accumulating prison sentences may become an avenue to prestige. This transvaluation of values has often taken place with the help of religious leaders, who are supposedly specialists in defending law, order, and traditional morality. Punishments long regarded as sanctions for right conduct come to be accepted as status symbols by revisionist groups. As modern colonial areas have won independence, those recently behind prison bars have often shifted their addresses rather directly to the residences of prime ministers or heads of state. For large numbers of ordinary citizens during days of reform agitation, being found guilty in the courts and sent to jail is no longer a mark of disgrace but a badge of distinction. The result is both legitimization and intensification of revolt.

In all these respects sanctions against the resisters come to have a negative effect. Instead of achieving their intended end of enforcing conformity, they contribute to the opposite result. This is like thrusting so hard to spear the steak on the other man's plate that one's own steak goes slithering to the floor. Policies calculated to weaken the resisters may actually contribute to their strength. This then becomes another of the social situations in which a deterrence policy does not deter. Under such circumstances, resort to brute force invigorates the movement aimed at. Insofar as persecution deepens dedication and group solidarity, this is again a demonstration of how it is possible for the blood of the martyrs to become the seed of the church.

During this early period in the pattern of nonviolent resistance, these phenomena are largely confined, however, to the resisters themselves. Other groups related to the struggle tend at this stage to become more intransigent. The typical reaction of opponents in increasing the severity of penalties has already been noted. The initial reaction of the general public, standing between resisters and their direct opponents, is also likely to be more hostile.

In addition to whatever vested interests of subpublics may be involved, there is likely to be a general shock that the *modus vivendi* should have been disturbed and especially by methods so unheard of. Any social innovation, including methods of change, carries a certain burden of proof. Since normally our more usual methods of educational or political action serve our needs tolerably well, the more extreme tactics of nonviolent resisters easily awaken unfavorable connotations of "radical" or "crackpot." It is probably true that the early effect of nonviolent resistance is not to win converts, but rather, to increase the number of those standing in opposition. (Of course, this is likely to be true of other methods also, including war. Any action toward a contrary goal influences the opposition to mobilize.)

It is not so widely recognized, however, that there are aspects of nonviolent resistance which for some persons tend to prolong this initial hostility. Nonviolent resisters have placed great reliance on the efficacy of their method in softening the opposition. The extent to which this occurs will be discussed in the next chapter. But although the awakening of sympathy will there be shown to play a part, it is not the only factor. Even beyond the initial stages, some opponents retain or deepen their zeal for repression.

This buildup in brutality may be the result of normal and rather rational goal-directed behavior. To the opponent, social order or the approach to social welfare through existing institutional arrangements may be goals of great importance. The only way to protect these purposes may seem to him to be the defeat of the resisters. Since, so far as he knows, the only way to accomplish this defeat is to increase severity, he quite understandably becomes more repressive. This seems to him to be the best possible expedient among the choices available, since all other courses of action involve evil also. Therefore, as a righteous man the opponent does what he ought to do, that is, he does the best he can. His evaluation of goals and of the consequences of his action may be wrong, but given his presuppositions, he is acting in a rational, defensible manner.

Emotional distortion as well as substantive analysis easily becomes involved, however. This is much more widespread than the occasional sadist who may be found in a mob or in a position of authority. There are such men who derive an intense satisfaction from torturing others. A much more common reaction, however, is that of the opponent who feels that he has been acting altruistically toward the resisters. Within a paternalistic, imperialist framework he may have expressed considerable kindness to a subject race so long as its members stayed "in their place." He may even have thought that he was requiring participation in God's own true religion, an essential to the eternal salvation of the resister. It is a disturbing experience to have this supposedly benevolent relationship disrupted, and to have the recipient of one's favors label as "bad" what was advanced as "good." When resisters rebel against what opponents considered to be a loving relationship, and themselves claim to be acting in love, this may enrage the opponent. He has seen himself as an exemplary person, graciously dispersing goodies in the role of a benign Santa Claus. Then the nonviolent resister, by his manifest suffering and by his emphasis on self-purification, makes the opponent's egoism dramatically clear. When anyone strips away our cherished self-images and exposes what we really are, he invites punishment. To keep on feeling like Santa Claus, we must demolish those who undermine the feeling. When Jesus compared self-satisfied religious leaders to "whitewashed tombs" (Matt. 23:27), he prepared the way for crucifixion.

The opponent, in his deepest heart, may know that his critics are right. As he stands behind the stool of a mistreated sit-in participant, he knows that he ought to be doing something to help. But since he cannot face the social stigma of helping and hates himself for his weakness, he easily lashes out at the resisters, insisting that the police or even the mob deal with these "disturbers of the peace." He knows that the resisters are right, but he cannot bear the knowledge. Therefore he represses it and strikes those who irritate his conscience. In the Bible are many illustrations of persons confronted with a difficult demand who tried to justify their inaction by punishing the prophet.

Psychologists commonly agree that frustration is likely to trigger aggression, even though it does not necessarily do so in every instance. When measures taken against resisters have proved ineffectual, and when an opponent faces a personal loss of status or threat to his personality, he may lay on all the harder. Feeling powerless and being unable to tolerate such a feeling of impotence, he resorts to force to give himself the illusion of strength. Or he may act the more aggressively because he subconsciously recognizes the justice of the resister's position or the benevolence of his attitude, and knows that the resister should win more support. Or a portion of the public may feel blocked by entirely different social conditions, such as low wages, a totalitarian ruler, or a nagging wife. Through the device of displacement they may find in the resisters a convenient scapegoat—an apparently safe group on which to vent aggressions, since the practitioners of nonviolence are both socially despised and will not strike back. Under all these circumstances rational social goals are forgotten. Only feelings of frustration and hostility remain to support greater severity and violence. Conflict then becomes an end in itself. The goal sought is only incidental. Satisfactions are derived from the aggressive act as such. Aggression then becomes self-feeding, almost regardless of what response may be made by those punished.

The opponent's interests are threatened by the demands of the resisters. His dominance is challenged, and often by persons of lower social status. We tend to be fiercely possessive of our wealth and status. We easily justify our defense of privilege by whatever rationalizations seem to identify our personal desires with the social welfare. Serious threat to our privileges and to our rationalizations produces anxiety, or chronic fear. Both experimental psychologists and anthropologists have observed that men under intense emotional insecurity tend to rely on habitual responses. Their awareness of other possibilities is reduced. Traditional reactions are seen as the only alternative. Even when these policies prove to be self-destructive, the only change that seems available is to use more of the same. This blinding effect of threat may be a factor in prolonging and intensifying the repression directed at resistance movements.

Another factor grows out of our cultural norm, which approves strenuous, aggressive self-defense, with physical force if necessary. We expect a man to stand up and fight back. We are trained to look down on those who are not "manly" in their response. When the nonviolent resister accepts suffering on himself rather than inflicting it on his opponent, he is easily classified as a weakling. He not only seeks an unacceptable end, but he uses a decidedly unconventional method. Opponents are the more ready to punish him since he violates our social code which says that it is virtuous to strike back.

There is a rational element involved here. Insofar as non-violence is interpreted as a sign of weakness, it "makes sense" to increase hostile pressure in the expectation that this will cause collapse of the resisters' cause. There may also be an irrational accompaniment supporting the reaction of some opponents. Some persons are basically cowardly, but put on an outer show of bravado. When they see action which they interpret as weakness or cowardice, they strike out at it as though despising it wholeheartedly. Not being able to strike at the weakness in themselves, they hit the harder at the resister. For such persons the sight of suffering endured may become provocative. Nonviolent resistance brings out the bully in those inclined to be bullies.

A number of these responses are likely to be accompanied by a feeling of guilt, which further distorts action. Even though the opponent is convinced of the purity of his aim in suppressing dissent, he may find himself using methods (beating, imprisonment, or perhaps killing) which even on the conscious level he knows to be reprehensible. In particular, he feels even more guilty when the person punished does not strike back. To maintain his self-image of decency he ought to be reducing the punishment. To repress the resistance campaign he feels it necessary to increase the punishment. He has been able to protect both his self-image and his cause only by some form of justification for his repressive action. Yet as the campaign moves on, consciously or unconsciously, doubts are likely to develop about the adequacy of the justification. Perhaps he really should not be punishing. But he has too much emotional capital invested in his policy to admit that he has been wrong. He finds himself in the position of the minister who shouts the louder where his argument becomes the weaker. When the opponent doubts the defensibility of terror, he may intensify it as a way of convincing himself that he was right all along. He may beat the more to try to avoid a feeling of guilt for those already beaten.

Suppression may be more severe when it is imposed by a group. Individuals then see their actions supported by an "in-group" whose approval they consider important. Personal impulses to violence are justified by the standards of the group. Private inhibitions are reduced; a group morale is built up by constantly supporting interaction. Hiding behind the barrier of institutional decision can insulate a person from emotional involvement. In conflict situations, many persons can act with greater intransigence as representatives of a group than they would as personal antagonists. They then apply different standards to conduct than those they accept for personal relationships. It seems easier to sin in syndicate.

For all these reasons the path of the nonviolent resister moves through intense conflict. Some of the factors just discussed are more characteristic of poorly adjusted or neurotic personalities. Others apply, at least to a certain extent, to any opponent. The history of nonviolent resistance shows that such patterns of intensification do emerge, and in varying degrees for different groups in the opposition. To win significant change, those normally apathetic must be aroused. Accomplishing this requires a vigorous and convincing presentation of a definite position. This inevitably threatens those who are opposed to the change. Not to arouse opposition is not to arouse support.

We need more research on conditions that tend to minimize the destructive aspects of conflict intensification. What more specifically is it in the strategy of nonviolent resistance that tends to arouse irrational opposition? What might resisters do to make it more likely that opponents would respond constructively? These are items of unfinished business on the agenda of scholarly research.

We do know that some opponents are likely never to be converted to the position of nonviolent resisters. If the method succeeds at all, it must succeed in spite of the fact that diehard opponents have not changed. A survey of further stages in the process will demonstrate how this becomes possible.

3

RESOLUTION AND RECONCILIATION IN THE RESISTANCE PROCESS

In the dynamic movement of a successful campaign of nonviolent resistance, the buildup of conflict and aggression that tends to drive groups apart eventually begins to turn toward a resolution that draws persons together. In unsuccessful or abortive campaigns, these next stages do not develop fully and the resisters finally abandon or postpone their efforts. Whenever the process does move through its full course, however, it is during the later periods that the unique consequences of nonviolent resistance become particularly apparent.

Up to this point chief consideration could be given to the resisters and their direct opponents. Now an increasingly significant part is played by third parties or observing groups. The contest between the persistence of resisters and the severity of opponents is decided not only by the tactics and staying qualities of these two antagonists. It is also influenced by the shifting allegiance of bystanders. The central social factor affecting the outcome is whether there is a sufficient detachment of support from opponents to force a modification of their repressive policy.

This description of the second major stage in the natural history of nonviolent resistance is deliberately worded. Not all the opposition needs to be converted. Diehards may remain of the same opinion still. They may also continue to be quite noisy and troublesome about expressing their opinions. It is not necessary to have a revolutionary overturn of the structure of society, replacing governments or social leadership—although if basic institutional issues are involved, this may be one of the long-run effects. Those who detach their support do not necessarily even come to immediate substantive agreement with the goals of the resisters. They may have been partially or fully converted, or they may only have come to oppose further persecution of the degree of severity that had developed. They only need to prefer to have the resisters doing what they have been insisting upon, rather than to pay the social costs of continued repression. In any of these cases opponents are immobilized. They no longer command enough support to maintain their previous policies. Resisters, on the other hand, are liberated to carry on more freely the activity that will finally win their goal.

Such detachment of support is significant since any social authority depends partially on the consent of the governed. This is true both of governments and of private organizations. In democratic situations this is quite clear. Dictators, to be sure, rely to a greater extent on coercion. A greater detachment of support is necessary in order to immobilize the tyrant. Yet even totalitarian systems must to a certain extent have at least a tacit endorsement. Every orderly system depends on some popular cooperation with leadership. Withdrawal of this degree of submission threatens the system, creating a potentially revolutionary situation. When they have lost sufficient support, leaders must abdicate or make concessions.

The Gandhi movement showed numerous illustrations of Satyagrahi action winning supporters from the opposition. Shridharani reports that he "saw scores of policemen and hirelings of the government refuse to harass or beat or trample nonviolent resisters who broke the salt monopoly in 1930."[1] A group of soldiers were court-martialed in the frontier province after they had refused to fire on a mass meeting of Gandhi followers.[2] Twice in Shridharani's own experience he "witnessed his co-workers' being sentenced by their own fathers who were judges in the British law courts. In one of the two cases, the son's imprisonment was quickly followed by the father's voluntary resignation from the bench and his subsequent participation in the very activities he had once penalized as a dispenser of justice."[3]

In one instance a group of demonstrators was met with a *lathi* charge. The Satyagrahi leader, a huge Sikh, was hit again and again until blood began to drip from his head. A particularly heavy blow felled him on his face. With a grin he stood up to receive some more. The police sergeant drew back to strike a final blow. Then he dropped his arms to his side, and said to a nearby newspaper reporter: "It's no use. . . . You can't hit a bugger when he stands up to you like that!"[4]

During the salt Satyagraha, many in the Bombay English community were reported to be appalled by the brutal police methods. Even some who a short time before had insisted on the necessity of British rule were taking the position, "Well, if the Indians are so determined to have dominion status as all this, let them have it and get on with it."[5]

During the periods of harshest punishment of the woman suffragists in Washington, protest meetings were held across the country, and many objecting letters were sent to the authorities. Dudley Field Malone, who said that at first he had been irritated by the picketing,[6] resigned as collector of customs for the Port of New York because of the treatment given the pickets.[7] Other prominent individuals, such as Judge Ben Lindsay[8] or Amos Pinchot,[9] opposed severity toward the women. Various congressmen, including some who opposed woman suffrage, became indignant over the way the police handled the pickets.[10] The Washington *Herald* summed up the difficult decision of many responsible citizens when it said, "Between the zealots of a progressive cause, and the scatterbrains who make their excesses the excuse for a lot of maudlin frippery, public opinion in the end must throw its support to the former."[11]

In the Massachusetts Bay Colony the sufferings of the Quakers aroused sympathetic expressions from numbers of colonists. The jailer's fees were repeatedly paid by sympathetic citizens or food was brought through the jail window at night.[12] At one of the executions, Edward Wanton, an officer of the guard, was so impressed by the bearing of the martyrs that he came home saying, "Alas, mother! we have been murdering the Lord's people."[13] He later became a member of the Society of Friends. When Horred Gardner prayed for her persecutors after her whipping, a woman spectator was so affected that she said, "Surely if she had not the support of the Lord, she could not do this thing."[14] Michael Shafflin, when asked by the court how long he had absented himself from orthodox worship, answered, "Ever since you put the servants of the Lord to death."[15] A large group of colonists seem to have been willing to legislate the death penalty only because they thought it would never have to be imposed. A special guard had to be posted to preserve order before and during executions.[16] Finally, popular support had declined to the point that the laws had to be made more lenient.

A shift of a few centuries to a different social climate and another problem does not alter the general reaction to repression and voluntary suffering. A restaurant owner in Cambridge, Maryland, panicked under the pressure of a sit-in. After seeing himself on television kicking one demonstrator, and smashing an egg on another, he reportedly said: "It was disgusting. I was wrong. Yes, I was. I'm ashamed. I'll never forget it. It makes me feel very little, less than a man."[17]

In order to support the lunch counter sit-ins, a picket line was placed outside a Harlem variety store. The person selling Bibles in the store came out to tell a picket leader: "You're losing me business like crazy—but don't stop. I'd even join you if I didn't have my concession here." Then he added, "I guess people have been reading my product lately."[18]

Leslie W. Dunbar, executive director of the Southern Regional Council, said of the sit-ins: "Not the least of their results was the effect they had on the white South. At first annoyed, then angered, then confused, white Southerners in scores of places came fairly rapidly to a grasp of the rightness of the protest. For almost the first time in their history, they yielded on a racial issue without being compelled by the federal government to do so."[19]

Again, support might be detached not necessarily because of developing sympathy for the cause of the resisters, but merely because of opposition to drastic measures for repression. The Atlanta *Constitution,* for example, illustrated the latter reaction in criticizing the lack of police action to prevent violence toward the freedom riders. "Either a community is going to believe in civilization or it is going to revert to the jungle. . . . Any man in this free country has the right to demonstrate and assemble and make a fool of himself if he pleases without getting hurt. If the police, representing the people, refuse to intervene when a man—any man—is being beaten to the pavement of an American city, then it is not a noble land at all. It is a jungle. But this is a noble land. And it is time for the decent people in it to muzzle the jackals."[20]

In the swing toward more sympathetic regard for the resisters and their rights, it is possible to speak of a spectrum of potential support. There are varying degrees of readiness to shift support, both among general observers and also among active opponents of the reformers. This continuum ranges from those individuals and groups most predisposed to alter their position, through various intermediary groupings, to those most rigid and tenacious in their condemnation of the resisters. In any society a number of internal differences and conflicts are superimposed on each other in a complex pattern. Persons react differently to the same situation because of their age, sex, class, political party, economic interest, ideological commitment, personality type, or numerous other distinguishing characteristics. There is unanimity of opinion on almost nothing. On social issues in particular, there is a changing pattern of constantly shifting alliances. A working majority on any given issue is a combination of various publics whose interests and convictions overlap at that particular point.

Some groups are more susceptible to particular types of influence or innovation than are others. Wherever there is social heterogeneity, there is differential receptivity. A certain number of persons stand in a unique relationship to the innovator. Relatives and friends, for example, are likely to be among the first persons moved by the suffering of the nonviolent resister. As they stand closer to him in intimacy of fellowship, so they also are nearer him in the spectrum of potential support. Also among the first to shift their influence are liberal groups, whose opinions in general are closer to agreement with the resisting movement. Examples have been anti-imperialists in England, religious liberals in Massachusetts, or strong believers in civil liberties forming judgments about conscientious objection in wartime. These groups are not eagerly standing in line to enlist in the resisting movement, but at least they are more likely to speak out in defense of the rights of minorities.

Then there are dissatisfied groups having other grievances against the authorities. Such groups may well be glad to see the authorities embarrassed or threatened by the resisters. To this extent they are allies in a common antagonism toward "the powers that be." Among the illustrations of those so loosely tied to repression have been those without the franchise in Massachusetts, or the opposition Republican Party during the suffrage agitation. Or without this degree of focus of their enmity, there are others who are more generally dissident or disaffected. Disequilibriums within the social system cause discontentment and frustration for some. These become marginal men with respect to the frustrating aspects of culture. They are more willing to break away from group norms at those points. They may direct their aggression at existing authorities rather than at a scapegoat. They more easily believe that a change might benefit their circumstances.

Between those working for change at one end of the social continuum and those most actively opposing it at the other lies a vast body of persons who on a given specific issue normally remain apathetic and indifferent. This includes the uncommitted group that answers "no opinion" on public polls. Or, even more commonly, its members may give only minimal support for a popular opinion they hold without much conviction. They are not deeply dedicated either to existing conventions or to proposed innovations. They refuse to get excited about the resistance cause, and neither do they think it important that the resisters be repressed. When the project of repression becomes nasty or annoying, they withdraw their support.

Such, for example, was the growing body of merchants who came to Massachusetts primarily for commercial reasons. On business matters they undoubtedly had genuine convictions, but they formed an influential group that was not interested in either the Quaker way of life or in maintaining an established church and political theocracy. In modern times, in spite of the myth of the "solid South," there is abundant evidence of a surprisingly large group of persons ready to swing in whichever direction vocal and respected leadership calls them. The number ready to invest sizable segments of fortune and sacred honor in last-ditch defense of customary ways is comparatively small. Considering the size of the total population, recognizing the encouraging climate often provided by top political leaders, and knowing that agitators and firebrands rush to trouble spots from a wide area, the surprising thing is that opposition mobs are as small as they are.

This is to be expected even in situations of far-reaching change. The percentage of the population deeply involved in determining the decision tends to be comparatively small. A certain French abbé was a prototype for the vast army of men in the middle. Asked what he had done during the Revolution, he replied, "I survived." The generality of men normally accept the situation as defined by respected leaders. Particularly since much leadership is likely to reflect the existing culture, any reform group still faces a Herculean task. Yet the number of persons in the spectrum of opinion that must be converted is not as large as we might anticipate.

At the opposite extreme from the resisters, opponents of the reform are also trying to win over the shallowly committed group in the center. This opposition segment of the spectrum can also be ranged along a continuum of intensity of conviction. The most reactionary among them are the least likely to be moved. For example, the most orthodox of the Puritans prodded the authorities, "heating" them to their work. Winston Churchill spoke out against more moderate government policies toward India. In 1931 he opposed even negotiating with "that half-naked fakir" Gandhi, although the outcome of the conference meant no more than the very modest concessions of the Gandhi-Irwin Pact. In the current civil rights battle a portion of Southern political leadership may prove to be the most vehement and least flexible of all the important opposition. As was pointed out in the last chapter, the severity of some individuals among the diehards may actually feed on the suffering of the resisters.

Opponents must be prepared, however, to see their sterner repression hasten the process of detachment of support by moderates. Every additional brutality helps to convince those on the fence that resisters are right in charging their adversaries with intransigence and extremism. As the enemies of the resisters become more violent, their friends become more numerous and more outspoken.

As it was helpful to portray the action of resisters as moving out through a concentric circle graph, so one can think of the counterthrust of opponents as moving through three concentric circles from (1) the kind of informal pressures constantly exerted by society toward conformity, such as mild ostracism or the indoctrination that comes from observing near unanimity in accepting "the thing to do," to (2) additional frequently used coercive penalties, fixed by law, to (3) more unusual, extraordinarily heavy, or little-used penalties, such as execution or extralegal mob violence. As repressive action moves through these types, at various places it passes the point of toleration for various groups in society. When enough such groups have reacted negatively, public toleration has been outraged. Then opponents, by the very methods adopted to strengthen their position, have contributed to their own defeat.

The situation created by the resisters may also stimulate support from third parties outside the immediate arena of the conflict. While Massachusetts authorities were struggling against the Quakers, letters of protest were sent by the governors of Connecticut and of Nova Scotia. Charles II of England sent the celebrated "King's Missive," throwing considerable weight on the side of the Quakers. Colonial leaders were anxious to retain a good reputation with the king and could not altogether ignore his authority. Yet royal intervention was scarcely a decisive factor in this case. The colony had a history of temporizing or ignoring unpalatable directives from the Crown. The missive arrived in November, 1661, after the persecuting policy had already been modified. Furthermore, a second letter from the king, permitting harsh laws against the Quakers, did not restore the full severity of persecution.

Similarly, in Gandhi's campaigns external influence may have been a contributing though not a decisive factor. In South Africa the resistance cause was supported by pressure from both Great Britain and India. Independence came sooner to India because the Satyagraha movement aroused public opinion in England and around the world. After the 1930 arrest of Gandhi, for example, 102 American clergymen cabled Prime Minister MacDonald urging him to yield. There were demonstrations of sympathy in other parts of the world also. One group, as a symbolic expression of support, even marched to the sea to make salt in New York harbor! Again in 1942, when full support during World War II seemed to require it, President Roosevelt urged Great Britain to come to a settlement with the Indian leaders. The pioneer sociologist, Edward A. Ross, described this aspect of nonviolent resistance by saying, "The weak get a change of venue from the will of the stronger to the court of public opinion, perhaps of world opinion."[21]

Contemporary civil rights protests in the South have also found outside support in other parts of the country. Numerous religious, labor, and general organizations have placed favorable statements on record. The business community has on occasion applied economic pressure from outside the area immediately affected. Federal law has proved decisive in local or state situations. The Montgomery bus boycott may well have registered gains in strengthening the morale of the Negro community, in preparing the local white community, and in shaping the national climate of opinion. But the act that immediately integrated the buses was not the boycott but a Federal court order. Under cold war conditions, antagonists in this country are also more sensitive to the pressure of world opinion. Morocco's *Al Fair* pointed out that the riots greeting the freedom riders were "compromising the U.S. position of world leadership." Many in this country also got the point when Radio Moscow said: "Scenes of bloodshed in Montgomery are . . . the worst examples of savagery. . . . They are particularly enlightening for . . . those countries where people of the Negro races and other colored people live."[22]

Detachment of various segments of influence from the persecuting policy of opponents reverses a previous process in the dynamics of nonviolent resistance. As was noted earlier, the first public reaction to nonconformity by the resisters is likely to be negative. When anyone goes beyond the bounds of tolerated behavior, society tends to be alienated from his cause. Both onlookers and direct opponents are initially likely to be repelled by the militant and unusual tactics of nonviolent resisters. During this early period the spectrum of potential support also seems to be significant, with action beginning, however, at the opposite end of the continuum. The groups that are most reactionary with respect to the proposed reform are the first to react in opposition to the strategy of nonviolent resisters. As soon as suffragists began their first comparatively inoffensive picketing of the White House, the National Association Opposed to Woman Suffrage hailed it immediately as "a menace to the life of the president—a silent invitation to the assassin."[23] It was not until several months later and after the appearance of more irritating banners that the opposition outcry became more general, including then many who were more favorably disposed toward woman suffrage.

A problem of the resister is to keep to a minimum the defection of support due to his nonconformity. At the same time it is a liability that he must accept. There seems no way to avoid some temporary strengthening of the opposition as a necessary step toward detaching support from the opposition. Resisting action must be unconventional enough to be repressed if suffering is to exert its power of attraction. The problem of the opponent is to checkmate the deviation by some tactic that will retain the support of enough segments of the population. The first impact of nonconforming action tends to solidify the ranks of the opposition and divide the supporters of reform between militants and moderates. The long-run effect in successful campaigns is to strengthen solidarity among the militants and to fragment the support of opponents.

After the initial strengthening of the opposition has been followed by gradual detachment of sufficient support from the opposition, the nonviolent movement is then likely to move into a period of notable acceleration of change. The first accretions of strength for the reform are likely to come at an agonizingly slow rate. After a certain "tipping point," however, progress speeds up appreciably. For the population as a whole, when enough power centers and opinion leaders have shifted their allegiance, it becomes "the thing to do" for their mass imitators also. At first an innovator can offer no status values in his new group. Later, status is attached to acceptance of the innovation. Then crowds clamor to climb aboard the bandwagon.

It may also happen within a single institution in society that interests dictate almost a simultaneous adjustment to a new situation. In economic life, for example, the first "equal opportunity" employer may be extremely hard to persuade. If it then becomes apparent, however, that he is losing little majority group trade and is gaining most of the minority group patronage, the customs of that entire line of business are due for rather sudden overhauling.

Or there may be advantages to be gained in being the first major group to cooperate with the inevitable. The earliest reformers face difficult days. If they can last through this bleak period and finally gain enough support to make it clear that the reform will soon be adopted in spite of remaining resistance, then the lines of the opposition are likely to break. Each opposition group may want to gain whatever lasting gratitude it may from helping to put the change across. The first woman suffragists, for example, suffered the hardships of the lonely nonconformist. As they finally approached victory, however, both political parties vied to gain credit for enfranchising such a large body of new voters. It became politically expedient to pass the Constitutional amendment. William Jennings Bryan urged Southern Democrats to vote for woman suffrage, lest their opposition handicap the party for the next twenty-five years.[24] One suffragist described the position of the major political parties in this jingle addressed to a fellow campaigner:

> Oh, Alice dear, and did you hear
>   The women soon will vote,
> For the elephant and the donkey both
>   Refuse to be the goat.[25]

Campaigns have differed at this point. The factors that make for acceleration may not always be significantly present. Minor concessions may, for a time at least, postpone rather than hasten a more massive readjustment. Nevertheless, resisters might well remember that it is entirely possible for the worst persecution to come shortly before capitulation by their opponents.

Campaigns of nonviolent resistance introduce unique elements for producing change in both opponents and third parties. These elements are partly persuasive and partly coercive. The coercive aspects will be discussed later. Insofar as the unique elements are persuasive, they are found both in the striking novelty of the nonconformity and in the suffering of the resisters under the repression by which opponents try to end their deviation. It is especially this suffering, voluntarily endured by those who continue to express goodwill, which introduces a new form of power into social relationships. If the action of the resisters is so "far out" as to be considered fanatical, the original strengthening of the opposition is never overcome. Spectators remain aghast at the radicalness of the campaigners. Even their suffering does not touch the hearts of those aware of it. But repeatedly in successful campaigns, when suffering commences, detachment of support from opponents also begins.

One of the distinctive qualities of nonviolent resistance is its more dramatic flavor, which makes for more effective publicity. As it was observed during Gandhi's campaigns, the tactics of nonviolent resistance "serve the same purpose as the electric lights on Broadway. . . . They advertise the passive resistance movement."[26] Reform groups normally depend on the familiar routine of pamphlets, speeches, and press releases. A public surfeited with these rubs its eyes and pricks its ears when demonstrations, civil disobedience, and imprisonment are added. These are newsworthy. The wire services and the television networks begin to spread the word to the world. When repetition has decreased the news value of a particular form of demonstration, resisters may introduce a new form of protest and again hit the front pages. The public is at least introduced to the issues through more inches of newspaper space and more minutes of prime TV time. Prevailing inertia is shattered and awareness is awakened. This makes for widespread discussion. If the reformers have a strong case, increased discussion is likely to be to their advantage. When the arguments are especially convincing on one side, the advocates of that side should be happy to have a more self-conscious analysis begin to replace a previous thoughtless acceptance of social custom.

The British Campaign for Nuclear Disarmament found that it was their marches and demonstrations which first broke the barrier of press silence and put them into the homes of the people. Especially when unusual suffering or punishment of prominent people begins, the news takes wings. After one of Martin Luther King's arrests, when he insisted on going to jail rather than pay a fine, the commissioner of public safety himself is reported to have paid his fine in order to get him out of jail. Before the announcement of his release came to them, King's followers were already making plans to hold a continuous prayer vigil outside the jail for as long as he remained in it.[27]

Nonviolent campaigners emphatically present new data to be grappled with by those receiving publicity. Both observers and opponents must somehow deal with this new content in relationship to their habitual thought patterns. For one thing they are forced to see that men have grievances so serious that they consider the suffering of resistance as a desirable alternative. In spite of weakened sensitivity and widespread satisfaction with the *status quo,* the public is forced to admit that men are suffering. Whether this is due to the general social situation or to the repressive reaction to protest, many observers are likely to recognize that they are somehow responsible for widespread discontent.

More than that, militant resistance helps to make clear the intensity of the desire for reform. When people are not only petitioning for the redress of grievances, but are willing to suffer for their cause, they must really mean it. Nonviolent resistance is a vast petition with life instead of pen. It is to be heeded the more because it is the shout of costly commitment, rather than the whisper of easy propaganda. When men carry placards in spite of *lathi* charges and police dogs, their slogan "Now" quite clearly does not mean "Somewhat later." Both sincerity of protest and intensity of conviction are validated by voluntary sacrifice.

Recognizing intensity of feelings is important to understanding a situation. It is not only a matter of X number of people who can be statistically tabulated as supporting a position. It is also a question of how deeply they believe in it. If a sociologist intends to register the social climate, he adds to his questionnaire some way of measuring intensity of opinion instead of merely counting noses.

Maintaining maximum social freedom also requires this degree of understanding. Democracy is not only a matter of protecting the liberty of decision-making majorities. As has ought to be allowed freedom for deviant speech and action. If the fullest possible regard for the rights of minorities. Insofar as it is at all consistent with the rights of majorities, minorities been illustrated in the Bill of Rights, democracy also means we are really concerned about maximum liberty, we ought even to be willing to allow a lightly held opinion, really considered inconsequential by the majority, to be outweighed by an intensely held conviction of a large minority.

When intensity is added to conviction, we ought to take the matter more seriously. We should move to make a more adequate response more immediately. When nonviolent campaigners are evidently giving a great deal for their cause, the rest of society does well to assign a higher priority to the issue. Not only is it in order to review previous conclusions on the subject, but also to reconsider priority on the agenda and the amount of energy to be expended in searching for a solution.

Nonviolent resistance tends to make a constructive reaction more probable because of the disarming quality of its approach. Any social controversy almost inevitably stiffens backs on both sides. Public disagreement on important matters introduces some rigidity into the situation. Both sides have made a social and emotional investment in their position. Neither wants to back down. Especially is this true if one feels personally threatened by others. Psychologists point out that reactions to frustration differ depending on whether the situation is sensed as mere "need deprivation" or as "personality threat." A threat to the security of the whole personality, or to the sense of individual status, increases the possibility of a strenuous defensive reaction. One probably learns very little if he feels personally assaulted.

The method of nonviolence tends to minimize this effect. Resisters at their best convey regard for antagonists and admit their own faults. They try to keep evil distinct from the evildoer, making their opponents feel they are loved and respected even while aspects of their action are being resisted. They try to understand the opposition point of view, insisting that they expect to learn from it also. Satyagrahis attempt to strengthen interpersonal relationships with the opposition. To a significant extent they take the suffering on themselves rather than inflict it on others. They may even perform unexpected acts of consideration and kindness. The reprisals that ordinarily accompany violence are reduced. The opponents' anger and belligerency find little to feed upon. Their position may be threatened, for nonviolent action is a powerful weapon, but they are not threatened personally. This inhibits the polarization which results in more intense conflict. Negative reactions are tempered. A more fluid and open situation is preserved. External threats normally tend to throw those attacked together in common defense. Nonviolent resistance in the long run tends to prevent this solidification of the opposition. Both direct opponents and third-party observers are comparatively more free to reconsider the data and to come to a somewhat more rational conclusion. Antagonists can change their actions without losing their identity. There is less threat to their selfhood.

Those who observe or oppose a nonviolent movement may also be led to review their positions because they come to hold an altered image of the resisters. Our response to another person is always shaped partly by the perception we have of that person. If we consider him responsible, capable, or morally worthy, we respect his opinions more highly, and we more often give him the benefit of the doubt. If our image of the other person pictures him as subhuman, immature, or hostile, it is easier to rationalize paternalism, exploitation, or punishment.

Human behavior is much more complex than a mere response to a simple stimulus. Our conclusions are distorted because we give selective attention to whatever we observe, on the basis of our particular backgrounds and desires. In a first glance at a crowded auditorium, a popular singer may observe the proportion of teen-age girls, but a fire inspector observes that there are only two exits. Among the intervening variables that stand between stimulus and behavior are our belief systems. When we see a group parading with picket signs down a main street, our reaction is colored by what we believe those men to be. We may applaud them as devoted patriots, or we may denounce them as dangerous agitators. Our perceptions are filtered through and distorted by the stereotypes we have attached to the group.

These stereotypes tend to insulate us from the complexity of reality. They become enclosing shelters shutting out the truth. The Quakers had been preceded to America by a greatly

exaggerated account of their character and behavior. Leading
citizens of New England saw them as libertines who danced
together naked, conspirators plotting to burn Boston and kill
its inhabitants, and heretics completely rejecting basic Christian
doctrines.[28] British imperialists saw the colonial peoples of
India as ungrateful recipients of the white man's bounty, incapable of self-government, backward in their customs, and
outrageous in their demands. Many of our contemporaries approach current campaigns for racial justice convinced that
Negroes are inferior, lazy, and stupid, and at the same time
content with their lot of separation and subservience.

A nonviolent campaign in many respects presents the resister
as a much different kind of person. It has been suggested that
in the United States today the letters N.A.A.C.P. might stand
for "Niggers Ain't Acting like Colored People." The stereotype
no longer fits the protest movement. Negroes quite evidently
are not all contented, lazy, or cowardly. Nonviolent resisters in
other parts of the world also have repeatedly been shown as
sincere, capable, courageous, and deeply concerned about high
moral purposes. For many persons this direct confrontation
contradicts previous images. When resisters act in unexpected
ways, their opponents must make some adjustment. By selective
attention they may see only what they want to see, thus protecting their false image at the expense of a repudiation of
reality. Some may even feel so threatened by an unexpected
response that they allow their insecurity to express itself in a
more intense aggression.

For those who are more open, however, images of the resisters
begin to change to accord more completely with reality. The
impact of dramatic demonstration and suffering, combined with
a comparative absence of personal threat, makes this outcome
more likely. Although perceptions always remain somewhat distorted, under these circumstances it is harder to maintain the
bias of old stereotypes in full force. It is easier to recognize at
least part of what so obviously exists. Under the conditions
created by nonviolent resistance, man's capacity for unreality
is more likely to be limited. Elaborate mythologies break down

before unavoidable evidence of mass suffering and of the personal integrity of resisters. It becomes really impossible for any except the most neurotic to say that things are still completely as they were once thought to be.

Settlement by negotiation then becomes more likely when the antagonists see each other as persons capable of conducting rational negotiations. A closer approximation to justice is possible when the beneficiaries of a situation in substantial numbers begin to recognize the reality of discontent and the moral worth of the discontented. When stereotypes have been replaced by a more adequate knowledge of real persons, a fuller and more genuine dialogue is possible. Negotiation then becomes encounter on deeper levels than was ever possible before. What previously passed for communication is then seen to have been the shallow mouthings of shadow men.

This fortunate outcome assumes, of course, the projection of this kind of image by resisters. This in turn depends upon the social maturity, and the moral and spiritual resources of the group. Saintliness in a single Gandhilike leader is not enough. The ruthless selfishness of traditional struggle over vital interests confirms stereotypes of enmity on both sides. Images can be modified only through a substantial expression of courageous commitment to a responsible goal and of unexpected goodwill toward opponents.

The voluntary acceptance of suffering by a group so characterized appeals not only to the intellect but also to the emotions of spectators. Many detach their support from persecuting authorities to a great extent out of sympathy for fellow human beings undeservedly put under the lash. Gandhi attached great importance to suffering as the language of the heart. Said he, "I have found that mere appeal to reason does not answer where prejudices are agelong and based on supposed religious authority. Reason has to be strengthened by suffering and suffering opens the eyes of understanding."[29] There is no limit to the suffering which Satyagrahis may need to endure. They must continue until suffering strikes a responsive chord. With a confidence born of personal pain, Gandhi said, "My uniform experience is that true suffering melts the stoniest heart."[30]

The sight of suffering may provoke a few to greater severity, but it moves many to more sympathetic consideration. The reaction to the bombing of Negro attorney Z. Alexander Looby's home marked a turning point in the successful outcome of the Nashville sit-ins. After the death of four Sunday school girls in a church bombing, President John F. Kennedy could well say, "I know I speak on behalf of all Americans in expressing a deep sense of outrage and grief over the killing of the children yesterday in Birmingham." He was accurately describing the wave of revulsion that swept over the nation.

Negley Farson once referred to Katherine Mayo's *Mother India,* with its influential recitation of exaggerated evils attributed to India, in connection with his journalistic descriptions of the Gandhi movement. He wrote: "The stories we had to send back continuously of the (apparently) brutal and needless beatings of defenseless Indians by British policemen soon caused the whole world (including England) to hold up its hands in dismay. They rubbed out *Mother India* as easily as you clean a child's slate."[31] A similar reaction was that of a Danish taxi driver who had enlisted to help transport Jews out of his Nazi-controlled country. His words were, "I don't know much about Jews, but this is bloody well against my religion and my morals—hunting people as if they were rats."[32]

In a free society at least somewhat colored by Christian values, we normally react against those who maintain concentration camps and gas furnaces. We develop new appreciation for students attacked by police dogs or cattle prods. We identify ourselves with men felled by *lathi* blows, or with the mothers of children killed in bombed churches. Martyrs hanged on Boston Common or idealists under persecution anywhere arouse our admiration.

Our cultural definitions are important bases for such personal reactions. Our society considers it important to eliminate the suffering of the innocent. This is not only a religious ideal for the faithful. It is also one of the commonly accepted decencies of life. One does not hit a man who is not hitting back.

One may restrain him for good cause, but one does not persecute him—especially not when he seems high-minded and even benevolent in his approach. In a particular community it may be considered proper to safeguard segregation, but it is not proper to jail praying ministers.

We are not equally concerned about the violent revolutionary. It is easier to justify violence against him, for he is also inflicting suffering and death. But when a reformer substitutes for violent aggression a philosophy of nonviolence, he adopts what Richard B. Gregg has called "a sort of moral *jiu-jitsu*."[33] The nonviolence and goodwill expressed by the victim causes the attacker to lose his moral balance. Unexpectedly he loses the moral support for his actions which he would have had if the victim had hit back violently. Under the novel circumstances of nonviolence, however, the general public—and perhaps his own conscience—will no longer support his repressive measures. Nonviolence has undermined the legitimacy of his customary response. The severity to which opponents resort as their strongest weapon now actually lends greater support to the resister's cause.

The power of suffering is a prominent theme in Christian tradition. Our concept of atonement relates the suffering of God to the redemption of men. Without pretending to go into the full nature and meaning of God's saving action, we can say that suffering love is God's strategy for dealing with evil. Only through the cross can men be redeemed without destroying their freedom. This is fundamental insight, related to the very nature of God and to the ultimate destiny of man. God saves through suffering. Or in the words of Berdyaev, "To conquer evil the Good must crucify itself."[34] Again and again, as men have stood at the foot of the cross with the centurion-executioner, they too have been brought to the transforming conviction, "Truly this was the Son of God" (Matt. 27:54; cf. Luke 23:46–48).

It is also the Biblical witness that suffering is the fullest expression of love toward fellowmen, and that such suffering in love contributes to the awakening and healing of others. Paul saw his own imprisonment as a support to his mission, both because it strengthened the faithful and because it became a witness to those outside the faith. "I want you to know, brethren, that what has happened to me has really served to advance the gospel, so that it has become known throughout the whole praetorian guard and to all the rest that my imprisonment is for Christ; and most of the brethren have been made confident in the Lord because of my imprisonment, and are much more bold to speak the word of God without fear." (Phil. 1:12–14.)

The death of the martyrs has always been regarded by the church as a most creative and powerful witness. From the Christian perspective, any listing of types of social power must include undeserved suffering in a righteous cause. Whatever its immediate effectiveness may be in the mundane turmoil of contradictory forces, every such dedicated expression of love lets loose some influence toward the transformation of the social situation. One of the most profound descriptions of this relationship is the fifty-third chapter of Isaiah. Both in its divine and in its human dimension the full meaning of vicarious suffering in service remains hidden in the eternal mysteries of God. Yet as a matter of historical fact as well as of religious faith, it can repeatedly be said of one who is "despised and rejected by men" that "with his stripes we are healed."

The process of nonviolent resistance illustrates important ways in which the dynamic power of suffering can be embodied in social movements. In summary, the dramatic novelty of the resisters' nonconformity and especially the suffering resulting from opponents' attempts to enforce conformity may help give wider publicity to grievances, validate intensity of conviction, minimize personality threat, change the prevailing image of the resister, and reinforce a sympathetic feeling tone toward him. In a society characterized by a spectrum of readiness for change, this may detach sufficient support from the policies of opponents that resisters gain their ends.

Thus far in this analysis, emphasis has been placed on the persuasive factors involved. It has been shown how convictions and feelings can be changed concerning the central point at issue in a nonviolent campaign. It must also be stressed, however, that important coercive pressures are involved in the outcome.[35] Both observers and opponents may come in effect to support the resisters, not because they have been converted to their position, but because they have been forced to do so on other grounds. Safeguarding their interests at these other points leads opponents to yield on the central point at issue, because they consider the other factors to be more important than the basic cause of conflict. They are simply trying to make the best of a bad situation and to accept the most advantageous outcome possible. They accommodate to unpleasant realities even though their opinions regarding the basic aim of the resisters remains unchanged or (since persuasive and coercive elements operate simultaneously) only partly changed.

Coercion has already been illustrated in those cases in which authorities back down simply because sufficient popular support has been detached from their repressive policies. They would prefer to continue the suppression, but they cannot do so and remain in office. Since they would rather remain in office than repress resisters, they unwillingly give up the repression. The effect of nonviolent resistance in persuading citizens has brought coercive pressure on political authorities. A similar coercive factor is involved in the filling of jails by resisters who court arrest. How many people can any government arrest? Not 100 percent surely, nor even 50 percent probably. When enough citizens feel sufficiently oppressed that going to jail, or worse punishments, becomes a badge of honor rather than a mark of shame, the coercive state is robbed of its power to exercise social control. Any government under such circumstances must either change its oppressive policies or give up its ability to govern.

Humanitarians in government or in the general population may oppose the cause of resisters, but also want to protect an image of themselves as decent, tolerant persons. In order to protect the second of these interests, they may yield on the first. For them the costs of terrorization and brutality have become greater than the costs of colonial independence, or whatever the resisters were contending for. Or opponents may be persuaded to the extent that they no longer consider the central issue to be as important as they once did. They may now see that victory for the resisters would not be as serious as they had originally thought. They would still like to have their own way on the central issue, but they no longer give as high a priority to this. They then conclude the sooner that continuing the struggle is not worth the trouble.

There may also be those who are more devoted to orderly community life than they are to defeating the resisters. They want Main Street quiet and are disturbed by the turbulence of continued demonstrations. Or parents who do not want racial integration may want even less to have the doors of the schools closed in the faces of their own children also. They therefore detach their support from repressive policies. Yet another group, extremely important in our society, finds it necessary to maintain business profits. When a boycott is part of a non-violent campaign or when demonstrations keep shoppers off the streets, they must balance the known loss that results from the boycott and from the demonstrations against the uncertain loss they feel would follow integration, if that were the issue. They may well come to deplore existing decline in business more than the presence of Negro customers or salesclerks. One discerning faculty participant in the sit-ins called loss of trade *"the one decisive reason* for the speedy success of the movement."[36]

When interests such as these are threatened, the controversy is likely to involve the power structure of the community to a degree never before attained in the previous conversations of interracial committees or community reform groups. More fundamental change may therefore follow this type of conflict and involvement than ever would have resulted in similar periods of time from gentler approaches. When deep differences exist, confrontation can remain pleasant and gentlemanly only if much is left unsaid, and if the most important issues are never dealt with in negotiation. Martin Luther King has put this quite realistically. "Nonviolent direct action seeks to foster such a tension that a community which has constantly refused to negotiate is forced to confront the issue. It seeks so to dramatize the issue that it can no longer be ignored. . . . The purpose of our direct action program is to create a situation so crisis-packed that it will inevitably open the door to negotiation."[37]

In addition to involving the community power structure in a more genuine facing of deeper issues, successful nonviolent resistance also produces a significant shift in the balance of power. The resisting group has demonstrated its economic, political, and social power to be greater than had ever been thought possible, perhaps even by the resisters themselves. Top community leaders must recognize a new status for a hitherto powerless minority. They are forced to modify their tactics accordingly. Again, Martin Luther King sees this clearly. In describing a lesson learned from the unsuccessful Albany campaign, he said: "We attacked the political power structure instead of the economic power structure. You don't win against a political power structure where you don't have the votes. But you can win against an economic power structure when you have the economic power to make the difference between a merchant's profit and loss."[38] It might be added that both dramatic resistance campaigns and methods supplementary to nonviolent resistance, like conventional voter registration, are likely soon to win the votes for Negroes that will be increasingly recognized by local political power structures also.

In all these cases, the total effect is due to a combination of persuasion and coercion. The strength of resisters includes both the power to persuade and the power to coerce. Politicians and businessmen might hold out longer and lose more elections and more profits, if their position was not being simultaneously undermined by a persuasive appeal. Many opponents are motivated not simply by a desire to choose the least unattractive pressure, but also by a recognition of genuine inequities that ought to be eliminated. They yield to coercion more quickly because their consciences have also been touched. This applies to the response of the general public also. One would normally expect that citizens would be so divided in conviction that a merchant, for example, would have to choose between compelling coercion from two sides. If he refused civil rights demands, he would face a boycott by integrationists. If he yielded reforms, he would face at least as serious a boycott by segregationists. In actual practice, the latter has frequently not eventuated, partly because segregationist sentiment has been sufficiently diluted or confused by persuasive elements that there is not enough moral fervor left to back vigorous, unpleasant action. The new situation is quickly accepted, and the merchant may come to see that he should have granted the reform much earlier.

One may conclude from such an analysis that the robust confrontation involved in nonviolent resistance wins its ends not by some esoteric mystique. Its dynamics can be identified by the scholarly methods commonly used by responsible specialists in religion and in the behavioral sciences. If its persuasive and coercive power proves to be sufficient in a given instance, the process moves on to a third stage, to a period of reform and reconciliation. After the earlier period of intensification of conflict, if there has been a second period of realignment of forces in favor of the resisters, then the third stage is marked by a readjustment of policies and relationships to accord with the new power pattern.

The transition to this stage may be marked by a definite crisis or turning point. This involves a break in the pattern of increasing severity of persecution by opponents and a convincing indication of willingness to negotiate or to formulate policy on a basis significantly more favorable to the resisters. An illustration of such a turning point was the passage of the Cart and Whip Act in the Massachusetts Bay Colony on May 22, 1661. Even hanging had not deterred the Quakers. Wenlock Christison was in prison waiting to be executed. Several others had returned from banishment and would have had to be apprehended and put to death if the previously existing policy had been maintained. Since the authorities lacked sufficient support to continue such penalties, they signaled a decisive modification in the Cart and Whip Act. This law still provided severe punishment. Incoming Quakers were to be whipped at a cart's tail from town to town out of the jurisdiction for their first three offenses. On the fourth occasion they were to be whipped out and also branded on the shoulder with the letter R. Not until the fifth offense were they to be banished on pain of death. This was a virtual abolition of the death penalty and was generally received as such. It marked the turning point toward declining persecution.

The crisis in the militant woman suffrage struggle might be identified as the commutation of six months' prison sentences in November, 1917. Even though penalties were not completely removed, the adoption of greater leniency, after severity had failed to halt the demonstrations, proved to be an admission by the authorities that they did not expect to stop militant activities. This act began the process of widening the area of tolerance to permit activities that could only lead to increasing success by the resisters.

A long-continued agitation, like the Indian independence movement, may have several campaigns of nonviolent resistance occurring at intervals. Each such major subcampaign may have its own crisis, as for example the Gandhi-Irwin Pact of 1931 or the complex series of negotiations that followed active resistance during World War II. The Gandhi movement became a series of surges toward final independence. As one Indian writer, B. Pattabhi Sitaramayya, put it, "The Satyagraha programme is not a D. C. (Direct Current) but an A. C. (Alternate Current) programme with 'make' and 'break' operating in alternation."[39] Or specific campaigns of nonviolent resistance might be regarded as thrusts of a jet engine turned on occasionally to accelerate more conventional methods of change.

The movement for civil rights in the United States has also included within it numbers of subsidiary campaigns, each with its own culmination, some successful and others not. Here too there has been a frequently recurring pattern of alternation. A particular campaign has reached a climax at which it appeared that a significant change in relationships had been secured. At this point a truce has often gone into effect. Demonstrations

stopped or were greatly reduced, while more serious negotiations took place or other mechanisms of political or social
reform were given time to register the new balance of power.
At times this has led to satisfactory change. At other times
these more normal procedures broke down or bad faith was
charged, and active resistance began again.

This suggests certain additional differences between nonviolent resistance and war or *coup d'état*. The latter manifestations of violence aim at a moment of victory, marked by a
crushing of enemy power, a final surrender, and complete
dominance. The nonviolent resister, on the other hand, is
more likely to define his purpose as victory for truth and his
attitude as one of appreciation for the opponent. He is therefore often content with a more gradualistic rather than sudden
approach and with a less thoroughgoing annihilation of opposition power. In these respects nonviolent resistance lies between
violence on the one side and the more common methods of
social change through education and political action on the
other side. The differences, of course, are not absolute. Some
instances of nonviolent resistance, as in the case of colonial
revolution, may finally lead to a drastic change in government.
War and revolution may involve a long series of slow campaigns, and they may be somewhat limited in their objectives.
At the other extreme, educational campaigns and parliamentary
procedures have their moments of crisis or breakthrough, and
they may result in major shifts in control, as for example in
the great Reform Bill of 1832 in England. In general, however,
without the excesses of violence, nonviolent resistance supple-
ments more usual nonviolent methods, speeding up the rate of
change and breaking down more obstinate barriers in the way.
It changes the climate in a way that makes possible more fruitful negotiation and more favorable civic decisions. A resistance
campaign may thus prepare the way and subside, while more
customary educational and political methods finish the job. This
again contrasts with war or revolution in which violence normally continues until the final capitulation. Full victory may
come some time after a nonviolent resistance campaign and as

a result of negotiation or parliamentary action. Yet the contribution of nonviolent resistance was essential to solidifying the resisters, changing the social climate, modifying the viewpoint of the opposition, and shifting the comparative power of the two sides.

After whatever turning point is involved in a specific nonviolent campaign, there is likely to be a period of uneven decline of repressive action, while opponents gradually accommodate themselves to the fact of surrender. There may be sporadic resurgences of persecution. Still reluctant authorities back down no faster than they have to. Or the resisting group may feel that it can gain an advantage by once again resorting to nonconforming action.

In colonial Massachusetts, for example, there were a few imprisonments and whippings under the Cart and Whip Act. In November, 1661, after the receipt of a letter from the British king, all penalties of corporal punishment or death to Quakers were suspended. Then in October, 1662, the Cart and Whip Act was reenacted, except that whipping was to be limited to three towns. About the time of the death of John Endecott in March, 1665, this fell into disuse. Later there were brief revivals of mild persecution, but no penal policy was administered with consistency and vigor. The last recorded whipping took place in 1677.

In the woman suffrage demonstrations in Washington, after the commutation of long prison sentences in November, 1917, the authorities adopted a cat-and-mouse system of repeated short imprisonments or fines. Some of the women arrested, however, were never tried, and finally a permit for the demonstrations was granted even though no application had been made. When the women began to build "watch fires," arrests were resumed, with regular sentences of five days in jail. This policy continued until, with the success of the suffrage amendment assured, demonstrations ceased in February, 1919.

In Montgomery, Alabama, after the first few days of peaceful acceptance of bus desegregation, there came a series of beatings and of bombings of homes and churches. Responsible elements in the community quickly reacted against such excesses. Bus service was interrupted for a time, but then again restored. Finally the disturbances ceased, and integrated buses continued to move passengers without serious incidents.

As the give-and-take of antagonistic struggle subsides, fuller fellowship between combatants is restored. Some legacy of ill will remains, as it does in all social conflict. Imperfect man does not yield power, nor gain power, as gracefully as he should. Some, scarred by battle, are never reconciled to the new order. Yet most men tend to accept the established reform, and most wounds heal tolerably well. Especially insofar as unique features in nonviolent resistance have maximized goodwill and minimized threats to personality, reconciliation is easier between resisters and their former opponents.

Whereas in earlier stages of the process, persistence and persecution interacted to build up to a crisis, now the movement is in the opposite direction. Retreat by their opponents tends to be matched by a less turbulent agitation by the reformers. As the authorities give up their opposition, the resisters moderate their perversity. The last years of the Indian independence movement were more characterized by negotiation than by civil disobedience. The militant suffrage demonstrations were terminated several months before final passage of the bill. In various campaigns pressure has continued unrelentingly up to the point at which opponents became ready to make significant concessions. Then there has often been a moderation in tactics so long as sufficiently significant progress was being made toward agreement. Settlement has then preceded further reconciliation in rebuilding relationships on a more cooperative basis. Although somewhat infected by utopian exaggeration, nevertheless a statement made about the Massachusetts conflict would seem to apply in general to successful campaigns of nonviolent resistance. In the contest between the Quaker and the Puritan, said William F. Poole, "the former amended his manners, and the latter his laws, or administered them more leniently, and finally they dwelt together in peace and harmony."[40]

4

THE ETHICS OF SOCIAL STRATEGY

An American newspaperman once asked Lord Irwin, the British Viceroy in India, what he thought of Gandhi. The Viceroy replied: "The first time I saw Gandhi I was tremendously impressed by his holiness. The second time I was tremendously impressed by his legal astuteness. The third time I was sure of it."

"Of which, Your Excellency?" asked the reporter.

Lord Irwin laughed and answered: "You've seen Gandhi. It's for you to say."[1]

The relationship between saint and politician in a single man, Gandhi, seemed decidedly obscure. Among contemporary churchmen, the relationship between professed ideal and concrete act is at least as incomprehensible. Even men of soundest intention have given little systematic thought to a coherent connection between the lofty norms incorporated in religious commitment and the practical judgments required by existing social and political situations. When one has seen a churchman, he is not quite sure whether he has seen primarily a Christian or primarily a reasonably decent reflection of contemporary culture. Occasionally, as when one writes a check for charity, there seems to be a suggestion of altruism. Or is this only astuteness in maintaining a public image in the suburb? Is the affability of the well-groomed executive an improved guise for the adventuresomeness of uncouth Biblical prophets? Does it reflect a better way of getting good things done, or a sure way of dulling the thrust of the best?

Men of sensitive conscience are continuously pulled apart by a confused tug of war between ethics and effectiveness, between principles and power, between what ought to be done and what can be done. This dilemma tortures us both when we ask where we want to go and how we can get there. Scholars have spent a great deal of time on the first of these issues. Although many questions remain, they continue to shed a great deal of light on social goals. At least in general terms there is a comparatively large body of literature on the improved patterns we ought to advocate in race, international, or economic relationships. There is much less research-based help available to us on the question of how we are to work for these desirable ends. We are therefore easily thrown into confusion by events like the contemporary Negro revolt. We do not really know how to evaluate boycotts, or mass demonstrations, or nonviolent resistance.

We are in the position of a man who is convinced that he ought to move to the other side of town, but does not know enough to call a moving van. Or it might be said that we are starving with a steak in the refrigerator, because the cook is on vacation and we are unwilling to reach for the cookbook. There is a fable which puts this well. A grasshopper was suffering so much during a cold winter that he went to the owl for advice. The owl immediately said: "Your solution is simple. Turn yourself into a cricket and hibernate during the winter." The grasshopper jumped joyously away, with all his problems solved—until he remembered that he did not know how to change himself into a cricket. He went back to the owl, who said: "See here, I gave you the principle. It's up to you to work out the details!"

We badly need a repertory of resources in methods of social change. To discuss only social goals and neglect means is not only socially utopian, it is an exercise in futility, assuming that wishing makes it so. Worse than that, it is also a truncated form of religion, leaving important aspects of life exempt from criticism by the Christian faith.

Delay in filling in the gap is now especially disastrous. We can no longer rely on the old method for getting things done when everything else has failed. This ancient last resort amounted to punching holes in people, by fists, spears, or bullets. This was quite the thing to do. Skill in it contributed to social status. The method was even blessed by leading churchmen. It was from the makers of church bells that men first learned to cast cannon. The earliest fieldpieces were often named after saints. As devout a man as Bernard of Clairvaux, in preaching the Crusades, cried, "Cursed be he who does not stain his sword with blood!"

While Neanderthal men in both church and state have not yet learned it, the dimensions of ultimate violence have now become so vast that we can no longer rely on the old expedient. Even in minor matters, with consequences that are less far-reaching, the efficiency of former methods is so low that they cannot satisfy modern demands. We have made striking progress in other types of means—in industrial processes and scientific research, for example. We can no longer afford to remain content with primitive means for social change. Comparatively speaking, our methods in human relationships are still often comparable to ox teams and oil lamps. What would happen if basic Christian insight were now applied as vitally to social methods as to social goals? What would it mean to us as change agents if love matured as rapidly in our total beings as technical skills have grown in our hands and brains?

Answering this question requires serious confrontation of the ethics of power, for power is the ability to achieve purpose. If the Christian faith is to inform our current dilemmas about method, power must come to be shaped and motivated by love. Yet love requires that this modification still leave a force that will be sufficiently effective under the imperfect conditions of the existing world. The saint and the astute politician must somehow be joined. Men with religious loyalties—and therefore with at least some friendly dispositions toward sainthood—have often stuffed the problem of power into the closet along with other skeletons they would rather not view. Perhaps it has been too much a reminder of our finiteness or a recall to an obligation so heavy as to be unbearable. Or perhaps we have thought that contact with power was contaminating and therefore unworthy of our pristine purity. Even while we have continued uncritically to use forms of power, we have hesitated to acknowledge the problem.

First of all, then, on ethical grounds one must enunciate the necessity and desirability of power. So long as we wish to move toward goals, we cannot eliminate power, for power by definition is the ability to gain ends. The use of power is essential if life is to be sustained or any other social goals are to be realized. Furthermore, this includes a variety of appropriate types of power. Occasionally someone acts as though we could dispense with all forms of power except for the moral attraction of the ideal, unaided by other human support. This is the mistake of the monastic. Or those with an anti-institutional bias sometimes suggest that religion would win more adherents without the church and without a structure for the evangelistic function. Those who long for the return of the day when the United States did not have such decisive world power may have fallen into the same immoral position. It is impossible to exorcise political devils with prayer alone, and we cannot win social ends merely with private physical calisthenics.

Those who overlook the realities of the power relationships of life are conjuring up an utopian never-never land that bears no resemblance to any spot in the universe. God himself is a center of power and is constantly demonstrating its high use for the achievement of purpose. A measure of power is one of God's gifts to man, to be managed with a sense of stewardship. Men who try to avoid complicity in the use of effective power are abdicating their social responsibility and rejecting their religious calling.

Projecting a visionary ideal situation without reference to the methods for its realization has only a limited virtue. It may involve the vice of suggesting that ideals have nothing to do with reality and that the virtuous man may participate in every manner of villainy if only his dreams are pure. Christian love requires effective means as well as righteous ends. While the strength of its proponent does not guarantee the righteousness of a position, lack of supporting strength does guarantee the defeat of a proponent, no matter how correct his theoretical position may be. There is no virtue in losing a cause by failing to match moral fervor concerning ends with prudent calculation regarding strategies. The children of darkness have frequently ruled the affairs of mankind because they were wiser in this respect than the children of light.

A second basic statement must also be stressed. Human power ought always to be subordinated to a sovereign God. As some would neglect power, so others would unduly magnify the place of power. Repeatedly there are resurgences of social philosophies which are so impressed with the indispensability of power that they would place power above principle. These would see in power itself an argument for the righteousness of one's cause. Both the economic buccaneer and the Nazi imperialist sharply reduced the role of moral controls. Nietzsche, in *Thus Spake Zarathustra,* expressed their philosophy by saying: "Ye say it is the good cause which halloweth even war? I say unto you: it is the good war which halloweth every cause." Hitler referred to "the eternal privilege of force and strength." Some hold the essential nature of the state to be power. The strength of the state then becomes the test of its legitimacy. For Machiavelli the state was devoid of moral obligation and was justified in using any means necessary to preserve its power structure. Even religion, said he, was a matter of vital importance to the ruler, not because it contributed to the common good, but because it was a most useful instrument for controlling the people and for using them as pawns in the real business of the state, maintaining and expanding its power.

This theory is still fairly popular among us. Its devotees include those who expect the church to become a loudspeaker system for whatever social philosophy may have dominant strength at the moment. Also worshiping at the shrine of power are those who rationalize from possession to moral right,

whether the ownership being justified is geographical territory, political privilege, or economic resources. Those who
assume that it is right to buy anything they wish so long as they
can afford it are placing the halo of power about unprincipled
desire. Those who argue that American economic strength con-
fers upon us the privilege of uncritical enjoyment of our resources come dangerously near to replacing an ethics of love
with an ethics of power. The assumption that the possession of
power grants the right to exercise it in the interests of the
possessor must be labeled for what it is, a pagan notion.

From the Christian standpoint power must always be subordinated to principle. Power is always to be regarded as a
means to an end, and the end is to be defined as the will of
God for the highest welfare of all men. So employed, power
allows man to participate creatively in the work of God. The
possession of power always carries with it the responsibility of
stewardship. The 1949 National Study Conference on the
Churches and World Order stated this well with reference to
the state. "We seek that our nation shall resist both the temptation to use its power irresponsibly and the temptation to flee
the responsibilities of its power."[2]

Biblical teaching is quite clear about this. The power of the
political ruler and of the economically wealthy is to be exercised
in obedience to God. Those with lesser degrees of obvious power
are called to make the same offering. There is sharp condemnation of those who use their strength for private aggrandizement,
and of those who see in their power any cause for pride or
self-justification. The appeal for dedication of the energies of
life is a demand for the surrender of power in obedience to God.

A third fundamental insight is that we are called to use
power within the existing world. Our immediate social vocation is not to be found in fifth-century China, nor yet in a
heavenly kingdom beyond present history. We are to act
responsibly at whatever spot we best touch the concrete circumstances of contemporary life. Love is concern for specific men.
Love is not irrelevant sentimentality. It is the willing of real
good in actual situations. At the same time that this defines the

arena of our service, it also places certain limitations on what we can do.

For one thing, we are finite men working with other finite men. We do not know all the possible uses of power. Our capacities are limited, and our judgments are clouded by past sin. We must therefore always act within a limited range of possibilities, and these do not include those perfect actions which would be possible if we were more angelic beings.

Power is a dangerous thing to place in the hands of finite man. Given man's tendency to act in his own interest, what begins as a responsible use of power may end as something quite different. Lord Acton's famous phrase is quoted even by those who illustrate it. "Power tends to corrupt and absolute power corrupts absolutely." The powerful are particularly prone to pride. They easily conclude that their strength is an indication of their virtue, and as Lord Acton warned, they may allow the office to sanctify the holder of it. Arrogant Pharisaism and smug satisfaction allow a confusion of private ends and public welfare. Especially when we have been successful, we more easily identify our own viewpoints with the ultimate truth. For this reason, victory as well as defeat presents fearful peril. Pride also tends to encourage rigidity of thought and intolerance of other views, which prevents full understanding of complex and changing situations. Power tempts us to preserve the *status quo* with whatever injustices it involves. What began as a subordination of power to justice then ends as the domination of power over justice.

Lord Acton also called attention to the tendency of power to expand indefinitely until it is met by a superior force. This is not inevitable. Power can be controlled by righteous direction. Yet power as such knows but one morality. Whatever preserves or increases power is considered good. When we concentrate on the increase of power, we tend to become preoccupied with the multiplication of means. This becomes our end, and we lose our original purpose, in the light of which alone did the means have value. Having accepted the necessity of power to achieve purpose, we may let power become our purpose. Ethical thinking then becomes a rationalization to support power. Morality is led captive, roped to the triumphal chariot of the conqueror. Having accepted the necessity of doing evil to accomplish good, we may come to call the evil itself good, which is the supreme triumph of the devil. We then attempt to use God as a means to support our power. We forget that we cannot serve two masters, and that might as well as mammon may become a competitor to God.

Not only do we ourselves as finite men face such limitations and temptations. In an interdependent society we are also always limited by what other men may or may not have done. Perfect social choices are generally impossible because the imperfect choices of others limit what can be done. On the other hand, better choices are possible because of the reasonably good choices others make. If others choose to join our reform movement, we can continue a mass campaign. If opponents choose to "liquidate" any friendly sympathizer, resisters must modify their tactics. If a population has a high enough educational level to understand the issues, we can conduct discussions on that level. If this background is lacking, we are forced to use less perfect means.

We cannot reach inside another personality and adjust the mechanisms of his choice to create an ideal climate—and even if we could, our own imperfections would still keep the climate far from perfect. We must act always under conditions that are partly defined by the choices of others. Because we are members one of another, sickness or health in any part of the body affects every other part of the body. In this respect also, "if one member suffers, all suffer together; if one member is honored, all rejoice together" (I Cor. 12:26). If one member perpetrates evil, all members must accomplish somewhat less good. If one member acts in love, all members find it possible to express somewhat fuller love.

This is further complicated by the fact that in any social situation, numerous values are always involved. All of these have a claim. No decision should be made on the basis of one alone. Yet usually it is not possible simultaneously to enhance all the values involved. A choice must be made that comparatively neglects one or more. We may consider both freedom and our economic calling to be important. If a tyrant should invade our country, we are forced either to surrender freedom or for a time to give up the vocation through which we normally serve society. Both freedom and "business as usual" cannot be equally served. Or, in any economy manned by finite persons, injustices are widespread. Somewhere in its progression from raw material to retailer, every product has been associated with some evil such as low wages or misleading advertising or unfairness to a competitor. In buying any economic product, we encourage the evil as well as the good policies that brought it to us, because we help make existing practices profitable. The alternative is not to buy, and thereby to starve. We are unavoidably involved in either economic injustice or suicide.

Further illustration is as near at hand as the last choice you made. To continue reading this book is to give up some other valuable enterprise in which the time might have been invested—and minutes once gone never return for reinvestment. (Surely this is a dangerous illustration, since it may result in an inordinate number of books being banged shut!) Other more general (and therefore perhaps safer) illustrations are the frequent conflicts between the claims of freedom and order, community and individuality, or short-run and long-run consequences.[3] Repeatedly we get either a good deal of value A and little of value B, or we get more of value B and less of value A. We are then compelled to accept an alternative that limits one value for the sake of the fullest possible realization of a system of values.

When our consciences are sufficiently sensitized, we see the shortcomings of common actions accepted by the generality of men as wholly good. We are then forced to admit that we are constantly using imperfect means. Because of the nature of man, the choices of others, and the complexities of values, the immediate full practice of the ultimate norm of love is impossible. Every available alternative is something less than completely ideal. The best that we can do is the best that is possible under the circumstances.

I have elsewhere shown that Jesus also shared this aspect of the universal human dilemma.[4] His ministry was limited by the weaknesses of the human material with which he worked (Luke 6:5; John 16:12). He thought it wise to give an ambiguous answer to a question that set a trap (Mark 12:13–17). He had to choose between ministering ceaselessly and getting required rest (Mark 6:30–46). For the best possible outcome he adjusted his plans because of choices made by others (Luke 13:31–33). Even the crucifixion cut short the real values of an earthly ministry at the same time that it let loose consequences immeasurably more important. Paul likewise worked within the limitations set by the opposition of many Jews or imprisonment by the Romans. He adjusted his own conduct because of existing attitudes, as in the case of eating meat that had been offered to idols (I Cor., chs. 8 to 10; cf. Rom., ch. 14). The Bible is such a valuable book partly because its characters shared the plight as well as the promise of the human condition.

Gandhi faced a modern counterpart to the same dilemma. The extent to which he made concessions to realism is often overlooked by those who are enthusiastic about his sainthood. If his devotees made a more adequate ethical analysis, they would see that his claims to sainthood are not diminished, but rather, enhanced by his efforts to relate an absolute standard to the necessary ambiguities of an existing world. The fact that Gandhi saw the need for political realism as well as religious idealism is not to be considered a defect in his character. Rather, it ought to be regarded as a virtue. If we believe that the good man should be immersed in the needs of the common life, then a social leader cannot be called a "saint" unless he is also a "politician" in the best sense of that term.

It has often been noted that Gandhi altered campaign strategy for the sake of practical effectiveness. Even serious students, however, have missed important points at which a healthy realism entered into his theoretical teaching. To be sure,

Gandhi continuously emphasized the importance of the ultimate ideal. Realistic concessions are much less evident in his writings. Nevertheless they are there.

Gandhi recognized that individuals on occasion ought to use violence, when their own resources of nonviolence had not been sufficiently developed. He wrote in *Young India:* "I do believe that, where there is only a choice between cowardice and violence, I would advise violence. Thus when my eldest son asked me what he should have done, had he been present when I was almost fatally assaulted in 1908, whether he should have run away and seen me killed or whether he should have used physical force which he could and wanted to use, and defended me, I told him that it was his duty to defend me even by using violence. Hence it was that I took part in the Boer War, the so-called Zulu rebellion and the late War. Hence also do I advocate training in arms for those who believe in the method of violence. I would rather have India resort to arms in order to defend her honour than that she should in a cowardly manner become or remain a helpless witness to her own dishonour."[5]

Gandhi saw circumstances under which a lunatic or a ravisher might need to be restrained. He said, "God would not excuse me if, on the Judgment Day, I were to plead before Him that I could not prevent these things from happening because I was held back by my creed of nonviolence."[6] In all these cases Gandhi regarded nonviolence as "infinitely superior" to violence. If one had enough mastery of nonviolence, it would be better to resist in that way. But if one's spirit and strategy of nonviolence were not adequately matured, he considered it better to act violently than not to act at all.

Gandhi was willing to kill dangerous animals. Although he continued to make a distinction between men and animals, he developed some important principles of social responsibility in connection with his discussion of animals. Gandhi wrote: "If I wish to be an agriculturist and stay in the jungle, I will have to use the minimum unavoidable violence in order to protect my fields. I will have to kill monkeys, birds and insects which eat up my crops. If I do not wish to do so myself, I will have to engage someone to do it for me. There is not much difference between the two." In connection with another person's killing a leopard that was threatening the village, Gandhi said, "To benefit by others' killing and delude oneself into the belief that one is being very religious and nonviolent, is sheer self-deception."[7] When a correspondent suggested that monkeys did not have to be killed because they could be kept off fields by a strong electric light at night, Gandhi replied that this would simply drive them to other fields, saving one man's crops at the expense of another's. To save society as a whole from "the mischief of monkeys," they must be killed. "The general rule," said Gandhi, "is that we must avoid violence to the utmost extent possible. Nonviolence for the society is necessarily different from that for the individual. One living apart from society may defy all precaution, not so society as such."[8]

Gandhi recognized the stubborn persistence of men's unreadiness for a completely nonviolent life. He therefore felt that a police force would continue to be necessary—even though, on the other hand, he also felt that an independent India could do without an army. He said: "A Government cannot succeed in becoming entirely non-violent, because it represents all the people. I do not today conceive of such a golden age. But I do believe in the possibility of a predominantly non-violent society. . . . No Government worth its name can suffer anarchy to prevail. Hence I have said that even under a Government based primarily on non-violence a small police force will be necessary."[9] On another occasion he said, "The police force will have some kind of arms, but they will be rarely used, if at all."[10] He did admit the necessity, for example, of killing someone about to commit murder, if the murder could not be otherwise prevented.[11]

In discussing the atomic bomb, Gandhi made the general observation, "While it would be absurd to say that violence has ever brought peace to mankind it cannot either be said that violence never achieves anything."[12] Considerations such as these led him to see the truth in a practical kind of relativism or situation ethics. He wrote: "In life it is impossible to eschew violence completely. The question arises, where is one to draw the line? The line cannot be the same for everyone. Although essentially the principle is the same, yet everyone applies it in his or her own way. What is one man's food can be another's poison. . . . Evil and good are relative terms. What is good under certain conditions can become an evil or a sin under a different set of conditions."[13]

If his teaching is taken as a whole, Gandhi did not oversimplify the problem of power as much as some of his followers do—or as much as his critics often claim that he did. A truly great mind holds together more facets of a problem than lesser minds seem able to do. Disciples have repeatedly transmitted only one, comparatively simple aspect of their master's teaching.

Enough has been said to show that in the use of power for social change, and in every other comparable choice, we select between shades of gray. We may daydream about being mounted on a white charger and jousting against a villain with heart of deepest black. The television screen or the politician's plea may portray situations in blacks and whites. This is the more easily done if one regards only one value or concentrates on only one goal. Actual social choices are more complex, with all the alternatives merely approximating the ideal to varying degrees.

A great deal of harm has been done, both within the church and within society, by those who paint only in blacks and whites. Such persons have a point in that important distinctions are surely to be made. Great differences do exist. These deserve emphatic description. But to exaggerate by denying genuine shortcomings on one side and real virtues on the other is both unscholarly and antisocial. Both theological and sociological illustrations abound. Quickly listing a number of them may serve to show how many of us are infected by such self-defeating oversimplifications.

Magnifying the distinction between Biblical and non-Biblical materials is one form of the fallacy of painting with blacks and whites. Actually, when we stop to think carefully, most of us would recognize that some Biblical materials are inferior to others, and that there are inspired passages outside the Bible that are superior to the worst in the Bible. Taking this shading of grays more seriously would make it easier to identify central Biblical truth. It would also make it more likely that intelligent modern skeptics would give sympathetic attention to the Christian faith.

We likewise handicap the Christian fellowship by an inaccurate black and white distinction between our faith and that of other major world religions. The only way we can maintain a long-run *absolute* difference between widespread religious faiths is to believe in one of two fallacies. We might attribute innate inferiority to entire peoples resident in other parts of the world, but this is manifestly false social science. Or we can imagine that God would withhold his full initiative from one part of the world but not from another, which is contrary to the revelation of love in Christ. Again, instead of a rigid dichotomy, we ought to recognize a continuum in which there are authentic revelations of God in other religious traditions and in which there are shortcomings in our human interpretations of the Christian revelation. This still allows us to assert a comparative, overall superiority for the Christian faith, and continues to command our enthusiastic evangelism, for the differences that do exist are still ultimately important and decisive. But to place our theology of missions on an oversimplified, untenable basis not only does serious damage to the Christian view of God, it also misdirects and actually obstructs the missionary enterprise. Both Christian theology and missions are too important to be so weakened.

The shallow expectation that choices can be made between unadulterated virtues and vices has also done a great deal of damage in social policy. A sharp dichotomy between criminals and law-abiding citizens overlooks a great deal of good in the "guilty" and a great deal of the criminal in the "innocent." Or we tend to see only good in our own nation or economic system, and only evil in an enemy nation or rival system. This poisons policy. It weakens our defense because we see only part of the threat. It postpones a solution to our problems because it neglects important possibilities for understanding and improvement. Social policy based on such shallow analysis easily embarks on utopian or reactionary crusades, marked by an extremist fanaticism that feeds the intolerance and inflexibility of the opponent also.

Oversimplification in methods includes the strategy of the militarist who trusts too much in physical weapons and denigrates all other procedures. On the other hand, the pacifist has often been able to see no good in more mixed strategies. He has sometimes been so concerned to avoid any compromise at the point of violence that he has compromised very seriously at the point of winning other ends. In evaluating nonviolent resistance, both sides have tended to underestimate the opposition position and to overestimate their own. This elevation of one's own opinion may contribute to a false sense of personal worth, or it may be a way of avoiding the labor of profound analysis and more sophisticated scholarship. Thereby social progress has been delayed, human values have been denied, and God's will has been left undone. Motivation may have been the noblest, but these are the kind of weakly implemented intentions with which the road to hell is paved.

This is one side of the picture. We diminish power by our unwillingness to be realistic about the circumstances under which it must be used. There is another balancing side to the total picture. We also perpetuate weakness in methods of social change if we merely continue the undue compromises that are commonly accepted. Under limiting conditions, God does not demand of us the impossible. He does, however, expect us to do the very best that is possible. When we recognize that all social choices are characterized by ambiguity, this does not wash out positive witness into a faded pattern of radical relativism. It is not true that every proposal is just about as good as any other proposal. To eliminate blacks and whites as available choices does not eliminate the differences between deep-dyed charcoal grays and off-white shades. In a given concrete situation there is an act that ought to be performed. It is the will of God under those circumstances. In a world that has come to embody both good and evil, God still fashions spiritual values of eternal significance. The meaning of life and the calling of the Christian is related to such a responsible use of the actualities of existence.

The ultimate ideal and present reality should always remain joined in a tight tension. That is, the ideal should be pulling decision as close to the norm as is possible, given the drag of resisting circumstances. Perfection always transcends any possible immediate achievement, at the same time being always relevant as goal, defining direction for choice. From the Christian standpoint then, power ought always to serve the ends of justice, defined as the closest approximation to the radical norm of love that is possible under the circumstances.

This becomes a critique of customary action. The generality of men in self-centered pride relax the ethical tension unduly. Widely popular current practices tend to be too great compromises. The thrust of Christian morality, therefore, always pushes us beyond the ordinary. There is a unique Christian contribution to be made to every situation. Although the responsible man never overlooks what exists in obstacles, he must always try to go beyond what already exists in methods and programs. Jesus and Paul were limited by their situations, but they also transformed those situations by extraordinary choices.

Precisely because the realist is aware of the demonic element in human nature, he should also be concerned about the quality of means. He will recognize the need to use imperfect means, but at the same time he should make certain that the means employed do not encourage or contribute unduly to the very sinful propensities he perceives. The end does not justify all means but only those which actually contribute to a greater good and for which there is no better alternative.

Insofar as even the best possible means involve imperfections, they always color the end obtained. Means are always ends-in-the-making. The outcome is never as good as it would have been if the situation had allowed better means. Evil always initiates its own chain of consequences. The limitations of the man and his situation are continued through defective means into the new situation. A parent may see nothing better on occasion than to coerce a child. This is not ideal. It contributes something to a negative reaction on the part of the child. Yet in a given situation it may be better than indulgence. If set in a framework of warm, accepting love, it may contribute significantly to the child's growth. The good in the act also releases a chain of consequences. Insofar as the initiative of the parent increases the amount of love in the situation and decreases the proportion of coercion, the outcomes of good in the means begin to overwhelm the consequences of evil.

Likewise the responsible citizen needs to recognize that under present human circumstances the authority of the state quite properly depends on both free consent and coerced compliance. At the same time he will go beyond accepted procedures in searching for novel, adventurous ways of strengthening persuasive elements and humanizing coercive elements. This applies not only to methods of social control, but also to forces for social change. Until we imaginatively incorporate into means the full measure of good that the social traffic will bear, social improvement is unnecessarily retarded. The question is, How, within given limitations, can we release more of love and less of hate, more of community and less of conflict, more of truth and less of obscurantism? Maximum power is to be found in the area of the possible, but at the point of the best that can be done. "All have sinned and fall short of the glory of God" (Rom. 3:23) must always be balanced by "You, therefore, must be perfect, as your heavenly Father is perfect" (Matt. 5:48).

Our most common fault is to make too little of the latter. We easily compromise too soon and too much. Given man's proneness to pride in past achievements and his desire for security through conformity to his group, we especially need vigorous challenges to more adventurous thrusts toward the ultimate norm of love. At the same time that we applaud Gandhi's healthy note of realism, we should even more applaud his perfectionist emphasis. Alongside passages quoted earlier in this chapter must be laid his expressions of supreme confidence in nonviolence and his insistence on purity of means. Since this aspect of his thinking has been widely publicized by numerous writers, multiplied quotations are unnecessary. A good summary of his position he put into these words: "Science teaches us that a lever cannot move a body unless it has got a resting point outside the body against which it is applied. Similarly in order to overcome evil, one must stand wholly outside it, that is, on the firm solid ground of unadulterated good."[14] This is the goal for all men. Complete eradication of evil is impossible without such a radical achievement. The strong statement of the ideal is to be taken as a spur to perfect oneself in the technique of nonviolence.[15]

Much recent research evidence in the behavioral sciences indicates that we can approximate the radical norm of love considerably more closely than we had thought to be realistically possible. The ways of our ancestors in several respects involved too much compromise ethically. Under present conditions they are also proving to be less effective sociologically. Educators, for example, whether they be parents at home or teachers at school, now rely less on the violence of the rod. They have found that discipline and growth are best achieved through a climate of understanding, trust, and affection. Emotionally ill persons are no longer normally locked into the punishing wards of a primitive "insane asylum." The modern psychotherapist knows the power of appreciative acceptance and has available a variety of more altruistic therapeutic procedures. Empirical studies in industrial relations show up the weaknesses of the violent battles of less than a generation ago. The specialist in industrial relations now tries to give a larger place to communication, problem-solving, and protection of mutual rights. Present-day criminologists see how the stern penalties of the past did not deter, but often trained persons in crime. We are coming to see that society can best be protected from crime through programs of prevention, sympathetic understanding, and individualized treatment. In international affairs, our best-informed leaders are advocating improved substitutes for nationalistic exploitation and civilization-threatening warfare. These substitutes involve more other-regarding concern and more peaceful forms of conflict resolution. The psychological and social sciences, in studying group relationships in general, are discovering a power in fellowship and mutual regard that once was considered at home only within the covers of the Bible.

The trend should not be exaggerated. The best methods in group relations are still far from morally perfect. The limitations of men still impose limits to what can be done. Yet it is now impressively clear that realism requires a tighter tugging toward the norm than the too-easy compromises of the past. We can no longer afford the tragedies that result from accepting the primitive practices of more Neanderthal days as the best possible. God is ready to show us how we can do better than that.

Only such a general theoretical exposition builds a solid enough foundation for the evaluation of methods of social change. It is now possible to become more specific in raising three questions that Christian ethics directs toward any particular use of power, such as nonviolent resistance. These are in addition to considerations, such as those of motivation or the quality of being of the actor, which apply to any human choice. Particularly relevant in evaluating social strategies are questions concerning consequences, agents, and inherent characteristics.

The first of these has already been touched upon. Any use of power should be evaluated partly in terms of the ends sought and the consequences actually resulting, since effects may differ from intentions. In which cause is the method enlisted? Is it an effective means toward that end? Does the importance of the end outweigh whatever loss (if it be only that of energy or time) is involved in the means? A mass campaign of nonviolent resistance might be justified to win liberty for an oppressed population, but not for quashing a traffic ticket. The significance of an act is related to the justice of the intended outcome. Undertaking civil disobedience against racial discrimination might be commended. Involving oneself in the same act in support of racial discrimination should be condemned. Instrumental values, such as demonstrations or political campaigns, acquire value chiefly because of the intrinsic value of the end sought. This requires also that they should be effective for their intended purposes. Power that is ineffectual or inappropriate is to that extent immoral. A sledgehammer is scarcely suitable for replacing the back of a watch. A toothpick will not dig a tunnel. These means have no ability to achieve the end sought. For these purposes, they are no longer power, but have become weakness.

On the level of social policy, the actual consequences of action are important in weighing alternatives. Some would deny this. They would rather say that the Christian is not concerned about calculating results, but only about responding to the will of God. The consequences he then leaves in the hands of God. Extreme forms of an obedience ethic stress faith in an immediate, intuitive awareness of the will of God, rather than emphasizing analysis or deliberation. It is difficult to see, however, how we can define the will of God on specific contemporary social matters without reference to outcomes.

The Bible is a guide to general directions, but issues like nuclear warfare, national health insurance, or lunch counter sit-ins are not mentioned in its pages. Appeal might be made to God's continuing revelation through mystical, intuitive experience, which we accept as self-validating. Taken alone, however, this is a dangerous guide, not because of any inadequacies in God's spoken word, but because of grave defects in man's receptivity. So-called "immediate" awareness is always mediated through the existing attitudes of a human personality. If God's intention is represented as blue, and man's bias as yellow, man's awareness of God's revelation becomes green. We too easily conclude that God wills what we want to do, or what our society defines as good. Even a saintly bishop caught up in contemplation finds it harder to accept that he should give up his special ecclesiastical authority. The generality of men, thoroughly indoctrinated in the virtues of capitalism, are less likely in their devotional moments to become thoroughgoing economic reformers. There is always a conservative tinge given by man to the radical revelation of God. Finite man needs all the help he can get in other openings to God in addition to intuitive awareness. In his goodness God has also granted man the capacities that make these additional avenues possible. One important check on the reality of revelation is the rational weighing of consequences.

Furthermore, the description of alternatives in concrete social behavior unavoidably introduces a consideration of consequences. If we are to give content to the will of God in the expression of love toward neighbor, we must ask what various actions actually do to the neighbor. Indulgent giving, for example, may be a bane rather than a blessing. It is a withholding from neighbor instead of a genuine giving. Even defining an act ordinarily requires consideration of some of its consequences. An act becomes murder when someone dies. Or, the distinctive intention in a boycott is that fewer goods should be sold.

It is understandable, therefore, that even those who theoretically reject the appeal to consequences do begin to use the test when they discuss specific social decisions. Unfortunately, they may still hesitate to use the full resources of the social sciences in helping us understand the effects of action. They too often base conclusions on common sense, or armchair considerations without benefit of more reliable data. Social scientists, on the other hand, professionally deal with only part of the full range of consequences. It is even more tragic if as citizens they do not add consideration of the more ultimate matters to which theologians call attention. Any adequate evaluation of the uses of modern power surely requires a comprehensive weighing of goals, material and spiritual, individual and social, long-run and short-run, as ends intended and as consequences attained.

A second ethical test for any particular use of social means has to do with the agents of action. Religious insight is also concerned about who exercises power. Obviously it would seem that those who can effectively use it for a righteous end have a certain claim to power. We ought to place the administration of resources in the hands of those who will manage them well. Any method that will help us do this deserves a certain preference. There is also, however, a less widely recognized consideration. The democratic principle, growing out of the Christian view of man, would require that suitable power be available to every man. All have an obligation to participate in the realization of the purposes of God and this requires the ability to do so. The nature of man as a being who is capable of growth through responsible choice requires that each have the power necessary for his highest fulfillment through service. This is a testimony against the consolidation of power, giving a disproportionate strength to any individual or elite class or nation, including our own. Sovereign power should reside in the people rather than in tyrants or paternalists, who always dominate, even though on occasion they may also aid.

Similar considerations, however, constitute a testimony also against a fragmentation of power, dispersing it among unrelated men or movements or nations in such a way as to allow them to act in isolated and irresponsible independence. A complete discussion of this point would be too lengthy for present purposes. It must be said, however, that under present circumstances the attempted anarchy of allowing persons or groups to remain independent centers of sovereign power leads to disorder and to increasing domination by a few. This denies the very rights of individuals which the anarchic system originally set out to safeguard. Instead of being either consolidated or fragmented, power should be shared by all in a coherent structure of community. This is the approach of democracy in which power is guaranteed to each individual within a framework of law. Every individual in the world ought to share in the control of some such community of power. All other things being equal, that method of social change is best which allows the widest participation.

A third moral criterion for the use of means deals with the kinds of power used. Different methods incorporate different inherent characteristics. These are important not only in relationship to the moral integrity of those using the method. A benevolent man contradicts his own nature when he uses malevolent strategies. The intrinsic natures of various methods are important also because they produce characteristic consequences. Previous discussion dealt with outcomes with respect to the end sought. These outcomes grew out of the appropriateness of the method for the intended goal. Here we deal with outcomes that result from the unique characteristics of a method regardless of the end for which it is used. Past experience with types of methods allows us to generalize and to predict that particular methods in themselves tend to do certain things to persons and to situations.

Social power appears in various guises and relationships. There is military power, appearing in wars and revolutions. Economic power is used in strikes, boycotts, or the allocation of capital. Political power is manifested in elections, legislation, or international negotiation. Propaganda and education use symbolic devices purporting to make some sort of rational appeal. Spiritual power is illustrated in prayer or mystical experience.

For purposes of evaluating inherent characteristics, these many manifestations of power may fruitfully be classified as either coercive or persuasive. (Some of the illustrations listed are general enough to include several elements, some of which are persuasive and others coercive.) The essential difference between coercion and persuasion is found in the reason that impels the opponent to act as the user of the method wants him to act. If the opponent acts favorably because he has been convinced and has changed his position with respect to the central point at issue, he has been persuaded. On the other hand, an opponent has been coerced if he continues to hold a contrary conviction, but nevertheless acts favorably only because he wishes to avoid some threat that is not inherently a part of the central issue.

Persuasion is illustrated if a man with ten dollars in his pocket reads a leaflet and exclaims: "I never saw that point before. This charity really deserves a ten-dollar contribution." He has internalized a changed attitude that will continue to influence future conduct. The transfer of funds would become an instance of coercion if a robber pointed a gun at the man, suggesting, "Your money or your life." In this case the "donor" would indeed decide that he ought to transfer ten dollars to the thief, but he would do so for reasons extraneous to those which he continued to think ought properly to determine the disposition of his goods. The robber compelled his assent rather than won his agreement. The reader of the leaflet will continue to contribute to the charity even after the leaflet has been destroyed. The victim of thievery will not continue to finance the support of the thief after the gun has disappeared.

The essence of coercion is attaching to one available alternative an unrelated and undesirable consequence in order to force adoption of another alternative. A driver, for example, may well consider the natural consequences of speeding to be the possibility of a car in the ditch and several days in the hospital. In deciding whether or not to exceed the speed limit he will balance the likelihood and seriousness of those natural consequences against the urgency of his errand. By introducing police action, however, society adds a coercive element. To the aftermath of speeding it adds a monetary fine or several days in jail. In the mind of the driver, "ten dollars or ten days" is not a natural consequence of speeding. It does not automatically follow, but it is a sanction arbitrarily added by human decision. Because of the legal penalty, a driver may decide to stay within the speed limit, even though he remains of a contrary opinion on the basis of the considerations he believes to be properly related to the central issue of appropriate speed.[16]

When persuasion and coercion are so defined, only persuasive techniques meet the full requirements of Christian ethics. The coercer does not completely deal with his opponent as a person. Instead, he manipulates him as an object. An attitude of love, involving deep respect for personality, would seek to protect the freedom even of those who disagree. It would try to create conditions within which men can act with unimpaired integrity. The full possibilities of fellowship are realized only when all participants can enter into relationship expressing their real selves.

Furthermore, truth is ideally best served by allowing full discussion of central issues rather than by terminating exploration by the use of extraneous force. Coercion involves a contest of power irrelevant to the point at issue. Might does not make right, whether the instrument used is the parent's paddle or the nation's bomb.

There are also practical objections to the use of coercion. "A man convinced against his will is of the same opinion still." When outer conformity is enforced and inner consent withheld, the person coerced is more likely to resort to deception and sabotage of any agreement reached. The process of coercion generates negative feelings and countermeasures. The opponent is more likely to feel justified in his use of similar measures, thus leading to a vicious circle of reprisals. The increase in the vigor and antagonism of opposition makes social change more difficult and tends to defeat the very ends for which the coercion is being used.

God does not coerce man with extraneous, arbitrary thunderbolts out of the blue. He maintains a situation of natural consequences that follow when men exercise their grant of freedom in particular ways. God does not compel any man's obedience or love. He provides a framework of conditions within which man acts, a standing ground that guarantees dependable natural outcomes. Within this creation, continuous loving persuasion is the dynamic action of God directed toward winning the assent of man.

Of course, man is not God. Our social choices are of necessity infected with ambiguity. A measure of coercion may often be involved in best possible action. In a given situation the weaknesses of coercion may still be less than the weaknesses of persuasion. Coercion should always, however, be kept to a minimum. It is to be used only when necessary to gain a greater value. The forms of coercion used should embody as much love and as little destruction as possible. Whenever we do coerce, we ought to be aware of what we are doing. We are compromising, and the burden of proof rests on every compromise.

It is helpful to distinguish also between two types of coercion: violent and nonviolent. Violence in this connection may be thought of as the direct use of physical force to injure or destroy persons or property. A strike, for example, is coercive, but it is not violent until beatings or sabotage of machinery enters in. In terms of its consequences, violence is potentially the worst form of coercion. Violence opens ranges of more ultimate devastation. Other forms of coercion limit human personality; violence can destroy the earthly person. It is true that limited forms of violence are less costly than the most serious forms of nonviolent coercion. A strike can drive a man bankrupt, which may be worse in its total consequences than breaking his jaw. A more legitimate comparison, however, is between the most serious forms of both methods. An employer would ordinarily see considerable difference between being bankrupted by a strike and being killed by a picket's bullet. Certainly boycotting a nation's goods would be preferred by most of its citizens to saturation bombing of the nation's population.

Employing the distinctions that have been made between persuasion and coercion, and between violence and nonviolence, methods of social change may be classified in three groups. These are: (1) persuasion, illustrated by various forms of education; (2) nonviolent coercion, including the strike and boycott; and (3) violence, such as war and revolution. Some forms of social power, such as political action or nonviolent resistance, involve a combination of methods that would be placed in different categories.

These three general groupings have been arranged in what would normally be a descending order of acceptability from the standpoint of Christian ethics. For reasons indicated above, the inherent characteristics of persuasive techniques are more consistent with the norm of love than are either of the other categories. Violence at the other extreme is the least satisfactory.

It is not a matter of indifference which type of power is used. Means are not ethically neutral. Persuasive methods ought to be given the fullest possible use in any panoply of power. In the modern world, violence can be used in only its most limited forms, lest the greater evil inherent in means destroy the possibility of any good remaining in ends achieved. Reforming groups are justified in moving down the scale to use successively nonviolent coercion and violence only insofar as these are necessary to achieve an end the value of which, in the balances of love, outweighs the losses involved.

This reintroduces the other major ethical criteria to be applied to the use of power. In addition to the types of power used, the Christian is concerned about the ends toward which power is directed and about the agents using the power. To summarize, the Christian faith cannot countenance the use of power for self-interest, or in unnecessarily destructive forms, or by monopolistic centers of control. Christian ethics calls for the fullest possible democratic use of united strength of the most creative types for the common good. Such a channeling of power becomes an expression of Christian love, a discharge of our stewardship over means, and an expression of our vocation.

Loyalty to these varied criteria in the realistic situations of contemporary life will require practical programs not all the elements of which measure up equally well. Utopian idealists sometimes argue that such a mixture of elements is contradictory and self-defeating. It is a program at war with itself. From the perfectionist point of view the consequences of the worst means used destroy the effectiveness of the best means used.

As was shown earlier in this chapter, however, life constantly requires mixed choices. In complex social situations there are different and contradictory factors to be dealt with. Dealing with the situation requires dealing with all its factors. To live in tension with any norm, then, necessitates a program that moves to a certain extent in two directions. Yet when such a program is well conceived, the weaknesses introduced by minor contradictions are swallowed up in the impact made by the thrust of the total whole. A strategy so composed of varied elements becomes the most powerful force available for a particular mundane purpose.

For example, if an airplane is being designed to meet public need, it should provide both space and economy. Yet elements planned to meet the two criteria work at cross-purposes with each other. Providing more legroom leads to higher costs. Looking forward to lower ticket prices requires cutting space per passenger. Somehow a compromise must be struck at a square footage that seems to conserve the best possible combination of both values. Similarly, no existing parent can bring up a child without some combination of coercive and persuasive approaches, even though these remain in tension with each other. No industrialist can long stay in business without a similar mixture of methods.

All human conduct involves a combination of good and evil. To act at all is to merge contradictory elements. For finite man to do the best that he can means that he will do better in some respects than in others. To argue that this is self-defeating is really to argue that life is not worth living and that the human situation does not allow the realization of spiritual values. On the contrary, it is the Christian faith that precisely as a person does immerse himself in ambiguous situations, salvation comes. God in the incarnation took on himself the liabilities of the human situation, not as a way of ensuring defeat for his purposes, but as a means toward overwhelming victory.

5

AN EVALUATION OF NONVIOLENT RESISTANCE

On August 27, 1962, seventy-nine religious leaders from various parts of the country went to Albany, Georgia, to support the civil rights resistance movement. On the next day they gathered in front of the city hall to pray. After only a few minutes they were arrested. Most of them were released on bail after a day in jail. Eleven stayed in jail and fasted for six days before being released.

A composite report was gathered from local Albany ministers by a national religious journal. The editors concluded that religious leaders in Albany viewed the prayer pilgrimage "with much disappointment." These pastors deplored the community tension that had resulted from the nonviolent demonstrations organized by Negro leadership, and they felt that the ministers' pilgrimage had only added to the tension, confusion, and ill will. In the words of the composite report: "Albany ministers feel that the pilgrimage participants could have done their praying at their home altars. If they had to make the Albany trip, they could have prayed elsewhere in Albany than on the sidewalk in front of the city hall. They need not have subjected themselves to arrest, their arrests accomplishing nothing."[1]

A Chicago minister who participated in the demonstration began his report by saying: "All around us, the bars of Dougherty County Jail formed hundreds of crosses. In our midst, our last clean handkerchief spread on a stained concrete floor became the Lord's Table. . . . The consecrated biscuit and grape pop tasted strange after six days of fasting. We silently recalled why we had come." He then goes on to say that they came in response to a genuine need to make an effective witness against an evil in which they too felt involved. He concluded, "We affirm with one voice that all this was God's doing, for it was not ours."[2]

These conflicting evaluations of a specific instance of nonviolent resistance were both made by ministers. These men, colleagues in a common calling, were presumably also equally sensitive and extraordinarily devoted to justice and goodwill. Nevertheless, they directly contradicted each other as to whether such an instance of direct action was "God's doing" or a confusing performance of misguided men. The evaluation of nonviolent resistance has frequently led to disagreement among competent scholars. It is one of the more controversial items in the field of Christian ethics.

Carrying through the general approach to social strategy that was sketched in the last chapter requires raising several questions about nonviolent resistance in particular. For one thing, where does the method stand in the descending order of ethical acceptability from persuasion to nonviolent coercion to violence? In the previous discussion of inherent characteristics of means, it was pointed out that persuasion ought to be given the fullest possible use, and that moving down the scale toward coercion and violence can be justified only as this is necessary to achieve an end that outweighs the losses involved in the method. How should nonviolent resistance be evaluated in this respect?

By definition, nonviolent resistance stops short of the use of violence. Actual campaigns have demonstrated that this is possible. Even in extremely provocative situations, where resisters have been sufficiently trained, leaders have been able to hold violent reactions in check. Wherever members of resistance groups have resorted to violent acts, they have done so in violation of the requirements of their method rather than as an outgrowth of its dynamics.

It may be argued that campaigners are responsible for unleashing the violence used against them by their opponents. It is true that resisters often stand for a reform so basic that it is bitterly opposed. They know that violence may result. Actual initiation of violence is still, however, due to the choices of others. Opponents are not forced to react violently, because other alternatives are available to them. As a matter of fact, the characteristic attitudes of nonviolent resisters are intended to make violence less likely. Resisters do not contribute to the violence latent in any situation of basic change where powerful, intransigent interests are involved. Rather, their total influence is directed toward reducing the amount of violent expression. Furthermore, when it does occur, they accept its consequences on themselves, rather than inflict it on others. Resisters are no more to be blamed for the violence of their opponents than Jesus is to be charged with perpetrating his own crucifixion. He might have prevented that too by avoiding Jerusalem and becoming a silent fisherman in Galilee.

In another respect, nonviolent resistance reduces violence by providing a substitute response for those who keenly suffer from exploitation and frustration. It is hard for the beneficiaries of a privileged situation to recognize the depth of the helplessness and pain felt by the disprivileged. Especially the extremists among those seriously deprived are likely to resort to violence if they see no other effective approach. Nonviolent resistance provides another possibility. It can become an emotional equivalent for rioting and a political alternative to revolution.

For all these reasons, nonviolent resistance is to be favorably evaluated for its avoidance of violence. As has been shown previously, however, it does not avoid all forms of nonviolent coercion. Resisters do not take all the suffering on themselves. They also impose some on others. The method tries to avoid associated feelings of hatred or pride, but it nevertheless includes coercive elements. Jawaharlal Nehru was even willing to say, "Often enough moral force is a far more terrible coercive

factor than physical violence." Speaking of the coercion involved in Gandhi's method, he wrote, "Whatever the motives
of conversion behind it, in practice it has been a powerful
weapon of compulsion as well, though that compulsion is
exercised in the most civilised and least objectionable manner."[3]

In any particular campaign the type of coercion used may
become more seriously destructive than is necessary or justifi-
able. Reducing a merchant's profits by boycott is one thing.
Driving him bankrupt is another thing. Believers in nonviolent action are likely to see such a difference as important
when coercion is directed toward themselves. They have, for
example, quite properly protested against driving share-
croppers off of farms, and therefore depriving them of a livelihood, simply because of their civil rights activity. Resisters
have been ready to accept reasonable jail sentences. At the
same time they might protest unusual or excessive punishment.
The same distinction, as they have often been ready to admit,
ought to be applied to their own activities.

Illustrations of coercion that might well have been considered unjustifiably excessive were Gandhi's fasts unto death.
The Indian Viceroy, Lord Linlithgow, went so far as to say,
"I regard the use of the fast for political purposes as a form of
political blackmail for which there can be no moral justification."[4] This statement takes in too much territory. It does not
use the term "blackmail" precisely enough. More important, it
overlooks the fact that a fast of limited duration, with a terminal
date set regardless of the action of the opponent, may have
quite proper political uses. Such a fast might well be a sincere
form of self-purification, an indication of serious dedication, or
a form of persuasion through suffering. When, however, a fast
is undertaken to continue indefinitely until specified demands
are met, this forces the opponent either to comply or to accept
the consequences of the death of as prominent and popular a
leader as Gandhi. It is difficult to see how this degree of unrelated pressure retains the disarming, reconciling quality that
is claimed as one of the superior features of nonviolent resistance.

Gandhi can be charged with inconsistencies at this point. Although he occasionally recognized coercive elements in his strategy, he tended unduly to restrict the instances in which he would admit this. He used some forms of coercion without admitting their nature. On the other hand, he usually drew the line at more extreme forms. He admitted that a degree of ostracism was called for against those who would not join boycotts of cloth. However, this was not to be pushed to the complete exclusion from livelihood of the offending person. He also discouraged picketing by sitting or lying down to block a passage, thus forcing opponents to stay out or drive over bodies. Such picketing he considered a form of violence. Yet his own fasts of unlimited duration would seem to have created just as extreme a dilemma for the opposition.

Nonviolent resistance has ordinarily involved less vehement assaults on the freedom of opponents. The method usually combines more limited forms of coercion with persuasion of a particularly potent kind. In the light of the analysis of the ethics of means in the preceding chapter, the use of such forms of coercion is not to be condemned. Instead, it ought to be counted in favor of nonviolent resistance as a social strategy in the existing imperfect world. The method is to be evaluated more highly both because of its realism about what is necessary in ambiguous human situations, and because of its insight into the self-defeating nature of excessive evil in means. Under existing circumstances it is right that coercive elements should be used. It is also right that they should be kept to a minimum, with the greatest possible stress being placed on forms of persuasion. As Reinhold Niebuhr well put it, the coercive factor in society is "both necessary and dangerous."[5] Either too great or too little reliance on it can be disastrous.

Some resort to coercion seems particularly essential in those campaigns for social change in which nonviolent resistance is justified at all as a supplement to more conventional methods. On social issues that are less bitterly contested, customary methods of education, negotiation, or economic and political action are sufficient. It is on matters of such basic conflict that important interests and stout resistance are confronted, that the extra power of nonviolent resistance is called for. It is this kind of issue which particularly necessitates some compulsion. Social groups seldom, or perhaps never, surrender major privileges voluntarily. If nonviolent resisters are to be criticized whenever they employ excessive forms of coercion, they should also be criticized when they use too little coercion to gain a sufficiently important goal. Not to use responsible pressure under such circumstances is to allow continuance of even more damaging evils, such as discrimination or exploitation or denial of liberty, and to make eventual resort to violence more likely.

Since some coercion is necessary where deeply rooted egoistic interests are involved, it is not surprising that some have opposed the use of coercion because they preferred to confine the use of nonviolent resistance to more superficial levels. Joining those who opposed coercion on more laudable grounds have been a few of more conservative social philosophy who did not want effective reform on more fundamental matters involving power structures. Nehru pointed out that in the Indian struggle, representatives of vested interests were among those who supported nonviolence because of their interest in preserving the economic *status quo*. By opposing both violence and coercion members of the ruling classes could find "the moral basis which they are always seeking in order to justify their special privileges."[6] They could feel a pleasant glow of righteousness in opposing coercion. At the same time, they could continue to enjoy power and privilege in a social structure that could not be altered without coercion. The presence of such persons in resistance movements illustrates again that politics makes strange bedfellows. Purists regarding method have sometimes been associated with reactionaries regarding social goals. However, the full form of nonviolent resistance, which includes coercive factors, has gained quite revolutionary ends. As a method, it is likely to prove disappointing to those who wish to limit the range of justice in order to protect their own prerogatives.

Especially in times when rapid adjustments are essential, nonviolent coercion may also be justified simply in order to speed up major change. Moving in the right direction too slowly may in the long run prove to be worse than moving in the wrong direction. Slow change may deceive us about our true condition. A democratic way of life, for example, moving at a leisurely pace on matters of racial justice, may be rejected by colored peoples of the earth, in favor of totalitarian systems which impress them as moving more rapidly on the single issue of race. It is possible that even a reactionary policy on race might in the long run lead to a better outcome for democracy, if it produced such a drastic reaction and shift in power as finally to bring about accelerated change. Slow change may be just enough to keep victims reasonably satisfied and to quiet the protest of their liberal friends, but not enough to meet the requirements of an era of rapid change in other areas.

This same general insight is suggested by the words of Jesus, "Truly, I say to you, the tax collectors and the harlots go into the kingdom of God before you." (Matt. 21:31.) Jesus was condemning the attitude of religious persons who had become complacent about being on the right road. He saw greater possibilities in those who, while on the wrong road, saw their error and speedily turned about.

Under some circumstances, in view of its full consequences, a slow rate of change may be the most immoral of all possible policies. So-called liberals may in this sense become the worst enemies of their own causes. Nonviolent resisters are quite properly concerned not only about the direction but also about the rate of change.

Another major aspect of the power of nonviolent resistance is primarily persuasive. Part of the inherent quality of the method is its reliance on "truth force." Gandhi felt he was releasing a new form of power in his "experiments with truth." Other resistance leaders have felt that their method allowed a larger place for rational processes in social decision. There is enough irrationality in man that no method can succeed—or even be attempted—with purely a rational appeal. Nonviolent resistance includes irrational elements, in distortions due to self-interest among resisters, in its coercive aspects, and in its emotional appeals to the sympathy of observers. In comparison with other methods, however, there is a greater possibility for the power of truth to commend itself.

Violence more directly produces victory for the mighty, who may not be at all identical with the righteous. It is true that reasonable war aims may help build morale, and therefore military strength. Yet war in itself cannot settle the question of truth or goodness. Unadulterated coercion has the same limitation. A bill may be rammed through a legislature by wielding the power of patronage, or a strike may be won by the side that has the greater economic resources and can hold out the longer. There is no "truth force" necessarily involved in such cases.

In several respects nonviolent resistance allows a more powerful presentation of a case under circumstances that keep persons comparatively more open to objective decision. By combining dramatic publicity with self-purification and suffering, nonviolence tends to reduce the rigidities and stubborn intransigence that often result from serious conflict. Both coercive and persuasive pressures can be exerted without provoking as much counterresistance from opponents and without forfeiting as much goodwill from observers. Avoidance of secret manipulations by resisters conveys the impression that they are willing to have their cause judged on the basis of its inherent appeal to the population. Emphasis is placed on communication and the desirability of negotiation. An intensity of conviction that makes a group willing to suffer stimulates other groups to review their position in the light of fuller data. Stereotypes tend to be broken down and the other side's situation can be seen with less distortion. Such receptivity to arguments other than one's own is essential to any more objective weighing of evidence and to any closer approximation to truth.

As has been previously shown, the outcome of a resistance

campaign depends largely on the direction in which third parties swing their support. They can judge resisters to be either admirable martyrs or misguided fanatics. They may consider their opponents to be resolute and righteous or to be cruel and unreasonable. On what grounds do they make their decision? Obviously on whatever grounds appeal to individual finite men in a particular culture. These include a variety of contradictory elements. It would seem, however, that reasonable decision plays a significantly larger part than is the case in other fundamental conflicts involving deeply rooted interests in power and profit. During nonviolent direct action, the general public does not simply observe which side is physically or politically stronger and award the victory accordingly. Rather, the public is brought to a greater extent to face the issues and to detach or shift support on the basis of what is considered to be right. Arnold Toynbee, in speaking of the civil rights protest in the South, concluded that the race problem there was being solved "by the force of conscience." Said he, "The fifth column that is sapping the Southern white's resistance to the doing of social justice is an awareness in their own hearts that their cause is not, after all, a just one."[7]

Nonviolent resistance tends to extend the advantages of free democratic discussion and decision into a range of problems from which these values are often absent. When the serious discontent of a minority has not been sufficiently impressed on the attention of the majority, the normal processes of public discussion are not activated. Or during revolutionary times, when fundamental changes are at stake, deeply involved self-interested groups are likely to resort to violent pressures and undemocratic manipulations, rather than to patient exploration of the merits of a case. Or, under dictatorial controls the usual procedures of public opinion formation and parliamentary action are not available. Under all these circumstances, nonviolent resistance opens the door somewhat wider to rational and moral considerations. To a greater extent it allows decisions to be made democratically, on the basis of what commends itself to the general population that stands between the resisters and their opponents.

In evaluating the inherent nature of nonviolent resistance, yet another major question should be raised. To what extent does the method involve a more radical expression of love to the extent of returning good for evil? Emphasis on this possibility is part of the ethical insight of major world religions. Does nonviolent direct action present a way of relating these neglected religious affirmations to practical social controversy? The Bible repeatedly enjoins: "Bless those who persecute you. . . . Overcome evil with good" (Rom. 12:14–21). Jesus was quite serious about his invitation, "Love your enemies" (Matt. 5:44). He illustrated this in ways that left little doubt about his general meaning. If we are struck on the right cheek, we are not asked only to endure it. We are to "turn to him the other also." If anyone takes a coat, the loser is not asked to "let him have it." Instead, he is to give away his cloak as well. If one is forced to go one mile, the word of Jesus is not "go cheerfully," but "go with him two miles" (Matt. 5:39–41). God continues his benevolent action, even toward the sinner. He destroys evil by transforming the evil heart with his goodness. We too are to find channels for releasing on the human scene this power of genuine love, expressed in both word and deed.

There are times, of course, when doing good to another requires that we not give him what he wants. Restraining him may be in his best interests. But this is not a complete answer to the ethical problem. There is still the question of how much we concentrate on the positive side of giving him what he needs, or how much we emphasize the negative side of withholding from him what he should not have. Or, is our primary intention to serve the other group or to win justice for our own? Do we rely on winning gratitude and building a loving relationship by contributing to opponents, or do we rely on coercion by withdrawing goods from opponents? To what extent should we build up opponents, or to what extent should we undermine them? Is it better to try to obliterate the enemy, or should we ever use group supportive methods?

Should one be more ready to denounce opponents for their evil or commend them for their good?

The difference in approach can be illustrated in numerous social situations. It has been suggested that workers, instead of going on strike, might continue working, but without pay, to call attention to their plight. In 1954 a group of Indian government clerks were reported to have decided to work two hours a day longer to support their wage demands. (The newspaper report raised some question about a formula for showing how much worse an employee would have to be treated to get him to work a desired amount of extra time!)[8] Lest we entirely discard the idea, we had better remember that parents often work harder and give more time and energy to a child in order to win a more cooperative response.

Nonviolent resisters have faced decisions about calling off campaigns when the opponent faces a serious emergency, or continuing them then in order to get additional coercive leverage by making the emergency worse. Gandhi at different times did both. He cooperated with the need of the government in South Africa and during World War I. He scheduled a major resistance campaign during World War II. An unanswered question among theoreticians of nonviolent resistance is whether occupying troops should be met with a social boycott as well as with political disobedience, or whether they might better be won over by fraternization and individual social cordiality.

David Riesman's earlier satirical article, "The Nylon War," has recently been reprinted as still relevant to a discussion of foreign policy.[9] In this fanciful tale he reported that the United States had been sending bombing planes over the Soviet Union, dropping nylon stockings, wristwatches, refrigerators, and other choice consumer goods. Among the consequences were consternation in the Kremlin, a more friendly attitude among the Russian people, and a counteroffensive of bombing Seattle with caviar, fur coats, and Stalin speeches about the minorities question.

This clever portrayal raises stimulating questions about the

uses of generosity for overcoming selfishness or of cosmopolitan-
ism for destroying nationalism. This is related to numerous
serious issues continuously involved in foreign policy. Can a
nation best increase discontent within another country by
pressures that contribute to the economic deprivation of its
citizens? Or can demands for a change in policy by an antagonistic government better be encouraged by demonstrating our
friendship toward its citizens? Or, how can we most effectively
gain disarmament agreements? Should we build our own
weapon stocks so high that it becomes too costly or dangerous
for an opponent to continue? Or by unilateral initiatives should
we make well-chosen cuts in our arms expenditures, indicating
that additional acts will follow if the other nation reciprocates?

The theory of nonviolence characteristically includes an
emphasis on returning good as a force for destroying evil. It
may be recognized that evil can be restrained by methods of
pressure, but it is also held that evil can be removed and
opponents transformed only by the healing power of love. Not
only ought a resister to bear suffering himself and avoid inflicting evil on an opponent. He should also give that which is
good in a testimony of practical kindness. Condemnation or
punishment tends to stir up rebellion, resentment, or defensive-
ness. Attack is likely to unite the opposition. A supportive attitude of psychological acceptance and positive expressions of
goodwill may divide the opposition, more quickly detaching
support from repressive measures.

Are such theoretical claims by resisters borne out in their
actual practice? The answer must be that they are only to a
limited extent. Not all followers are as saintly as leaders. Even
leaders, like the generality of men in our culture, spend much
time on the level of justice, balancing pressure against pressure,
rather than on the level of love, spontaneously meeting evil
with positive good. In spite of injunctions to love enemies,
morale seems to depend to a great extent on cultivating an
impression of the enormity of the wickedness of the "enemy"
and of the chasm set between an "in group" (the resisters) and

an "out group" (their opponents). Even Gandhi's followers showed a certain amount of glee at the discomfiture of their antagonists. They sometimes took delight in their own skillful maneuvering to get police to arrest them. Or they enjoyed the spectacle of police chasing those "raiding" a salt depot in the direction of the depot instead of away from it.

Yet there is also a significant difference in comparison with more predominantly egoistic methods of social change. Gandhi, in prison in South Africa, made a pair of sandals for Prime Minister Smuts. In a later essay in honor of Gandhi, Smuts said, "I have worn these sandals for many a summer since then, even though I may feel that I am not worthy to stand in the shoes of so great a man."[10] Satyagrahis in India on occasion shared their supplies with police who stood for hours blocking their way.[11] Quakers in Massachusetts spoke words of love, even though they were sometimes almost hidden by their other words of turbulent denunciation. Wenlock Christison declared to the court that condemned him that he had come "not in contempt to any of you, but in love to your souls and bodies."[12] Illustrating the reaction of others also, Horred Gardner, after being whipped, kneeled and prayed to God to forgive her tormentors.[13]

In more general ways resisters have taken care to avoid unfair embarrassment to opponents by their campaigns. Their group attitudes have often been characterized by genuine concern for those with whom they contended. As Martin Luther King put it, "In a world in which most men attempt to defend their highest values by an accumulation of weapons of destruction, it is morally refreshing to hear five thousand Negroes in Montgomery shout 'Amen' and 'Hallelujah' when they are exhorted to 'pray for those who oppose you.' "[14] In our cynical generation it is startling to realize that Negroes engaged in painful combat have, in their mass meetings, broken into applause after the reading of I Cor., ch. 13.[15]

The fact that nonviolent resistance offers only a partial illustration of returning good for evil might be used as an

argument in its favor. This may well be another illustration of
the well-balanced realism necessary in an imperfect world.
Facing actualities in himself, his children, and his culture, the
wise parent knows that he must both fix limits and build
relationships of trust and affection. If he relied only on winning
gratitude by continuous gifts, he would probably find himself
being taken advantage of by "spoiled" children. There are
times when giving the stolen candlesticks to the poverty-stricken
thief contributes to his reformation. There are other times
when the same act would simply confirm him in his thievery.
If this is true in the intimacy of the family or of person-to-person
relationships, how much more is it true under conditions of
cultivated egoism, blindness to justice, and reluctance to change,
which appear in mass society. In international relations, the
nation returning good for evil can be taken advantage of. Its
good intentions may feed aggression. The aggressor, having
been once successful, may take still more the next time.

Under such circumstances the spirit of the Sermon on the
Mount calls for the kind of resistance that is the best good that
can be done to all concerned. In his campaigns, the nonviolent
resister is also right in his active attack on evil, even though this
deprives the opponent of returns which under other circumstances the resister would be glad to give to him. In public
policy there is often a place for an iron hand in a velvet glove.
God manifests justice, in maintaining tragic consequences for
evil acts, at the same time that he also shows mercy.

It is not entirely sufficient, however, to explain away the
problem by distinguishing between sentimentality and a realistic expression of goodwill. It is also true that we do not put as
much good into our reaction to evil as we might, even under
unfavorable circumstances. We ought therefore to be grateful for
the touch of unusual benevolence involved in nonviolent resistance. At the same time, we might wish for more illustrations of
an even greater return of good for evil. No major group has
ever experimented fully enough with the possibilities here. We
remain essentially ignorant about the potentialities in what

might prove to be a major breakthrough in social relationships.

Up to this point in the chapter, evaluation of nonviolent resistance has dealt with the nature of the method. Another criterion for judging means is the question of who exercises power. As elaborated in the preceding chapter, there are dangers in both monopolization and fragmentation of power. We ought to give preference to methods that allow the democratization of power.

In this connection nonviolent resistance has a great deal to be said in its favor. We have seen important ways in which it gives a more effective vote to the voiceless. It is a method available to the common man. It has been used under totalitarian conditions when there seemed to be no other avenue for expression. As a supplement to usual forms of democratic discussion and decision, it provides a stronger voice to those whose influence is otherwise weak. This is true for several reasons. Those disenfranchised by various forms of discrimination can vote with their feet and their pain. Minorities can register the intensity of their feeling. Majorities find means for amplifying their voices when they have been too easily disregarded by centralized manipulators of power. The method allows groups at the grass roots, or the rice roots, to band together in movements that can match power elites and may become adequate for overcoming entrenched resistances to change. Yet this is more than a contest between extremes, since typically the decision is made by the direction in which the general public shifts its support.

There is, however, a strong counterargument advanced against all of this. One of the most frequently expressed objections to nonviolent resistance is that it takes a utopian view of the human situation and expects too much of man. Since men are incapable of the heroic dimensions required for difficult resistance or of the disinterested response expected of opponents, it is argued that nonviolent resistance is a possible alternative in only a narrow range of social situations.

It is true that many of the supporters of the method, insofar as they were at all theologically sophisticated, held a more optimistic view of man. They have tended to stress the doctrine of the image of God rather than of original sin. Some version of the Quaker view of the "inner light" has been taken seriously. As they saw something good in every man, so they have also insisted that there were some substantially right-thinking men in every society. They believed there were enough available resources of spiritual strength to support the perseverance, self-control, and devotion required of resisters. This emphasis also allowed confidence in enough observers responding to injustice and suffering that resisters could win their end.

Gandhi expressed such high expectations when he advised, "Even if the opponent plays him false twenty times, the satyagrahi is ready to trust him the twenty-first time, for an implicit faith in human nature is the very essence of his creed."[16] Or again, he said: "If you want to convert your opponent you must present to him his better and nobler side. Do not dangle his faults before him."[17] Although this stresses the potential nobility of persons, it also recognizes the reality of human faults. There is something in human nature that can respond to goodness. Every man has a capacity for high spiritual development. Gandhi placed his emphasis here. Yet he also saw another side to the nature of man. In discussing sex ethics, he observed: "Man unfortunately forgets that he is nearest the divine, hankers after the brute instinct in himself, and becomes less than the brute. . . . Man must choose either of the two courses, the upward or the downward, but as he has the brute in him, he will more easily choose the downward course than the upward, especially when the downward course is presented to him in a beautiful garb. . . . The downward instinct requires no advocacy, no argument."[18]

Such realistic features associated with nonviolent resistance have often been overlooked by its critics. Resisters have often been quite gloomy about the reactions of opponents. They have recognized that victory would often be difficult, that extreme amounts of suffering might be required, and that even then their efforts might fail. They have also listed decided human limitations among resisters. There is always a danger that the movement will get out of hand and become violent. Temptations to pride may corrupt resisters who have become newly powerful and are not accustomed to prestige or leadership positions. Even martyrdom may be an expression of human pride, or an attempt to build a posthumous reputation as a saint. Or men may not be willing to pay the personal price that is necessary. It is all very well to say that exploitation or tyranny can continue only so long as the oppressed cooperate, and that in this sense men forge their own chains. But nothing can be done about it if men would rather cooperate than be tortured.[19]

Since there are never enough angels to go around, students of nonviolent resistance have emphasized the need for training to make the most of more mundane material. A Z-3 resister is not much good against an A-1 opponent. A successful demonstration cannot turn into a mob scene. Therefore various devices have been used to release personal resources, to instruct in the procedures of nonviolence, and to develop group solidarity and control. These have ranged from the most informal to the quite systematic, including the service of worship of the early Christians, the social service programs of Gandhi's ashrams, and the role-playing sessions of the American civil rights movement. There has been some speculation about preparing entire populations in the use of nonviolence, as, for example, against invaders. In such a nonviolent society it has been proposed that appropriate education might be provided through public schools, churches, mass media, the counterpart of military maneuvers, and a nonviolent resistance staff college.[20]

One's reaction to these possibilities depends partly on his theological view of man. Accepting nonviolent resistance as a method does not, however, require a utopian view of man's potentialities. A more balanced view, recognizing in human nature God-given possibilities for both good and evil, is quite consistent with the mixture of coercive and persuasive elements in nonviolence. Even a more pessimistic view, placing considerable stress on man's bias toward evil, could allow enough possibility of response to God's grace to support limited uses of the method. Nonviolent campaigners do not have to be early candidates for sainthood. Neither, in view of what actually happens in resistance campaigns, do opponents have to exhibit great capacities for conversion. Gandhi was right in saying, "The weapon of *ahimsa* does not require supermen and superwomen to wield it; beings of common clay can use and have used it before this with success."[21] Certainly there is sufficient historical evidence to force one to admit that Indian peasants, untutored religious minorities, and Negroes from ghettolike slums have successfully manned resistance movements, and that a great variety of opponents and publics have responded with a degree of decency that has made the struggle socially worthwhile.

A third general question to raise concerning nonviolent resistance has to do with the ends gained. Obviously these ends may have infinite variety as the purposes of campaigns differ. Nonviolent resistance might be used to win colonial freedom or to defend a dictatorial government from aggression, to establish racial integration or racial segregation, to pass a law or to repeal the same law. No comprehensive evaluation of such specific aims is here possible. Judgment is necessary for each separate campaign.

There are certain concomitant consequences which tend to result from nonviolent resistance, which can be generally evaluated. These clusters of typical results follow the use of other methods also. Violence, for example, may or may not succeed in winning the specific goal toward which it is directed. Regardless of the outcome in that respect, however, violence leaves a deposit of physical destruction, ill will, and breaking of community. Nonviolent resistance also has typical consequences that deserve attention. Three alleged outcomes will be here examined: the social disutility of too frequent use, the moral growth of participants, and the cultivation of community.

Nonviolent resistance, especially when it is too frequently

used, may contribute to social turmoil. It is a kind of emergency action that should not become normal in an orderly state. Demonstrations filling jails are an improvement over riots, but they are still costly in terms of the ongoing processes of social life. For one thing, if it becomes customary for too many people to go to jail too often, the whole system of law, including wise statutes and progressive courts, may be expected to lose much of its effectiveness. In occasional campaigns this does not significantly follow, but a more continuous use of nonviolent direct action would be another matter.

It would also seem that if nonviolent resistance were used too often on too many minor issues, the method would lose considerable effectiveness. Much of its publicity value depends on its novelty. When a society becomes accustomed to seeing good people punished, it may no longer react with the same sympathy. Observers may remain apathetic in spite of suffering endured. At least any single tactic within the general method of nonviolent resistance may be subject to diminishing returns.

This problem of the social disutility of too frequent use of the method is illuminated by a brief consideration of the ethics of civil disobedience. This is not the place for a full discussion of that topic, yet a reminder of some of the chief features of the problem will help to define proper ends not only for civil disobedience but for other forms of nonviolent resistance as well.

Some would defend the authority of the state to such an extent as to deny any proper place for extralegal action. They would say that no individual has a right to act as his own legislature. Especially is this thought true in democratic states, where there are constitutional provisions for change. Some would also apply the principle to totalitarian government. They interpret Rom. 13:1–2 to refer not only to the general function of the political institution but to each act of every specific government.

This emphasis comes to grief on the rock of the basic Christian doctrine of the sovereignty of God. No human institution, including the state, is to be given a higher authority than God. "We must obey God rather than men." (Acts 5:29.) We accept the duty of civil disobedience when we assert the sovereignty of God over all forms of human government. To go along with grossly unjust law is to have other gods before the Lord. When we place ourselves at the disposal of God, this is not taking the law into our own hands so much as it is trying to place the law in God's hands.

Civil disobedience as a form of religious devotion has had an honored history through long generations of saints and martyrs. Many of those whom we now honor were in trouble with the law in their own day. Time lends perspective. In the warfare between conscience and conformity, we regularly disapprove those who practiced conformity. We could apply to church history as well as to our national background the words of Theodore Parker. Speaking against support of the Mexican War, he said: "Men will call us traitors: What then? That hurt nobody in '76! We are a rebellious nation; our whole history is treason."

We have learned to make the distinction described in I Peter 4:15-16. If a person is punished as a murderer or a thief, his act is to be counted as morally inferior to the law he disobeyed. If a person suffers as a Christian, he glorifies God, and the law is to be considered unrighteous. (Worse therefore than the conscientious objector is the ordinary citizen who disobeys laws he admits to be just—such as traffic regulations—yet would hesitate to disobey seriously unjust laws.) Law changes its moral classification depending on its content. The enforcement of some laws becomes a crime against God. Their violation becomes good citizenship. In the Nuremberg war trials we assumed that obedience to cruel Nazi regulations was immoral, whereas disobedience was moral. This discriminating reclassification of law by the moral man was illustrated in the case of the Fugitive Slave Law. After having been punished for violating it, Theodore Parker on the following Sunday said from his pulpit: "To a law framed in such iniquity I owe no allegiance.

Humanity, Christianity, manhood revolt against it." Henry Ward Beecher was even more explicit in his classification. He said, "But as for those provisions which concern aid to fugitives —may God do so to us, yea, and more also, if we do not spurn them as we would any other mandate of Satan!"

Disobedience of unjust laws in one respect contributes to performance of the function for which the state was ordained by God, and for which it also exists in political theory. The state is stimulated to fulfill its divine and constitutional purposes when its leaders know that men will refuse to obey if the state violates its proper aims. This is one implication of the words of Pericles to the Athenians that the secret of liberty is courage.

It can also be argued that civil disobedience to a certain extent contributes to respect for law in general, because resisters hold that ordinarily law should be obeyed, and because they expect that a penalty will be assigned for breaking the particular law they find unacceptable. They are not trying to undermine legal procedure as such. They consider it right that the provisions of the law for punishment should be observed. They are trying to improve the legal structure which they believe to be undermined by any seriously unjust law.

Even when all this has been said, it still remains true that civil disobedience should be used sparingly. If everyone constantly acted in accordance with all his minor preferences, we would have a considerable degree of anarchy. Gandhi, who spent a good part of his life in jail as a law violator, also saw the necessity of limiting the use of disobedience. Looking forward to an independent Indian government, he said: "I would be deeply distressed if on every conceivable occasion each one of us was to be a law unto himself and to scrutinize in golden scales every action of our future National Assembly. I would surrender my judgment in most matters to national representatives, taking particular care in making my choice of such representatives. I know that in no other manner would a democratic government be possible for one single day."[22]

It is true, of course, that resistance on a major matter of

conscience may necessitate drawing the line at what would otherwise be a minor point. A civil disobedience campaign directed at an important goal such as national independence, for example, may involve subsidiary acts of disobedience like making salt from a cupful of sea water. A larger campaign may be built on a series of tactical maneuvers, just as in war a soldier may give his life for the immediate object of capturing a hundred feet of shell-pocked mud. For those concerned about religious freedom, even a pinch of incense on the emperor's altar gains significance when taken in context. This does not, however, destroy the requirement that the more ultimate end of an act of civil disobedience should be a major matter.

This principle becomes even more evident when set within the framework of the central problem of political science, the relationship of individual freedom to state control. Any discussion of this problem should point out that the state has certain obligations. It should keep interference with individual freedom to the minimum necessary for protecting social welfare as defined by its citizens. It should maintain democratic procedures, allowing all to participate in policy decision. It should keep penalties for conscientious law violators as low as is consistent with the general purposes of the state. Having done this, however, the state has no option but to punish the nonconformity that is considered serious by majorities.

The individual citizen, on the other hand, also has important obligations. He should act contrary to state requirements not because of a self-centered personal whim or desire, but only when a sincere moral objection remains after careful review of his own position and examination of the arguments for the other side. He ought to consider the dangers that disobedience poses for the social order, weighing the evils of obedience against the undesirable consequences of his disobedience. He ought first to exhaust the possibilities in other nonviolent means of change, including education, negotiation, political and economic action. Having done all this, if he still feels he cannot conform to law, then he has an ethical obligation to follow his conscience and to stand ready to take the consequences.

It is in the right of the state to enforce law and in the right of the individual to act conscientiously that the problem of individual freedom and social control comes to its sharpest focus. The various qualifying obligations listed for the state and for the individual help to reduce the seriousness of the conflict, but they do not eliminate it. A study of the social process of nonviolent resistance suggests another observation that helps to resolve this central issue in social thought and practice. When a conscientious individual violates law and accepts the penalty, he is appealing to the power of "truth force." Punishment by the state may succeed if his and future generations continue to consider his deviant conduct as extreme, dangerous, or fanatical. He can also realize, however, that if his position proves to be commendable, his very suffering will hasten the time of its adoption by society as a whole. The very act directed toward defeating him then releases a new dimension of democratic action and an additional power resulting in his victory.

All these considerations reinforce an important conclusion about nonviolent resistance. The method is morally justified, but only when it is related to important ends, and when it is therefore used comparatively infrequently. Massive means should not be used for trivial ends. This point is clear with respect to war. It should also be clear with respect to major campaigns of nonviolent resistance. The latter are appropriate only when other nonviolent methods have proved inadequate. Nonviolent resistance ought to be used *as an alternative to violence and as a supplement to appropriate forms of education, negotiation, and political or economic action.*

Still another consequence of nonviolent resistance needs to be examined. This is the claim that it is redemptive for both sides, or that it contributes to the moral growth of all involved. Gandhi, for example, insisted that his method "blesses him who uses it, and also him against whom it is used."[23] Other thoughtful resisters have felt that this contrasts sharply with war and the harsher forms of coercion. These methods, which emphasize harming the other side, tend to brutalize all concerned. Nonviolent resistance, on the other hand, contributes to the ennoblement of both sides. Sole reliance on violence or coercion results in a descending spiral of reprisals and counter-reprisals that incites the growth of selfish ethnocentrism, pride, and belligerency. Nonviolent resistance substitutes an ascending spiral that encourages a broader interest, self-examination, and mutual regard. As violence undermines character and personality values, nonviolence enhances them.

It is easy for partisans of a position to oversimplify at this point. We ought to be reminded that along with its degenerative effects, even war evokes some heroic virtues. On the other hand, it has already been shown that nonviolent resistance does set group against group and does involve more manipulation of others than is often admitted. Furthermore, values claimed for it are shared also by the best conventional forms of persuasive communication.

All this having been said, however, there is still truth in the claim for mutually enriching features in nonviolent resistance. Certainly within the resisters themselves there have been nurtured resources of strength and courage which they did not know they had. These are called out partly by the situation into which resisters are thrust and partly by the training they undergo. Self-purification is not a part of most procedures for seeking social ascendancy—especially not of the comprehensive sort which has often involved cultivating the spiritual life as well as perfecting the tactics of a campaign. This helps to explain the difference between the morals of an army camp and those of a Satyagrahi ashram. Participation in nonviolent direct action helps to build up initiative, courage, group loyalty, wholesome self-respect, and determination to resist injustice. At its best the method stresses social, moral, and spiritual values, encouraging a disciplined nonattachment to material possessions and physical life.

This not only means that the sanctions of the opposition are less effective, since confiscation of goods, sufferings of the body, or even physical death are less of a threat. It also means that higher values are enhanced within the resisters whether their campaign is successful or defeated. Even though they may not "win" relative to their adversary, they may yet gain unsought by-products relative to personal character.

The dramatically revelatory impact of nonviolent resistance in the long run is likely to increase the number of participants who share these values. Numbers of previously passive by-standers are aroused to greater social responsibility. Their protective insulation from the throbbing realities of life is broken, and they are shocked into at least thinking about important issues. When the usually soporific television screen shows praying demonstrators being dragged to police vans, it is likely to be more moving than when it shows a political analyst sitting at a desk and deploring world conditions. As one college staff member said during the recent racial demonstrations, "This is the first time that Vassar girls have picketed in twenty years."[24]

Opponents, as well as onlookers in general, are presented with conditions that invite their growth. Not all respond, to be sure, but it is easier to do so than it is during the deeper hostility and threat, the secrecy and trickery of war or unadulterated coercion. This is especially true insofar as resisters succeed in their unique combination of positive goodwill with pressure for reform. If resisters can convince others of their limited objectives and if they can provide avenues for saving face, defensive, prideful reactions are less necessary to meet the ego demands of opponents. If reformers convey the impression of having the best interests of opponents at heart and reduce threat to personality structure as such, they become more disarming, leaving others more open to dialogue. When men take suffering on themselves, rather than inflicting it on others, onlookers are more likely to give a genuine reexamination to their own positions. Insofar as resisters show fearless devotion, unbiased willingness to learn and therefore to compromise in negotiation, magnanimity, and unexpected acts of kindness, onlookers and opponents can more nearly afford to live up to their own highest capacities for objectivity, sympathy, and generosity. Unearned suffering incurred in the service of justice can be redemptive not only for the sufferer and the observer, but even for the person inflicting the punishment.

Related to this is another concomitant outcome claimed for nonviolent resistance, in addition to whatever success it may have with respect to the central aim of a campaign. Proponents claim that their method is more conducive to community. A closer and more meaningful fellowship is said to be possible both during and after the struggle.

Again the claim should be stated in somewhat more modest terms. Nonviolent resistance creates cleavages too. Whatever fellowship follows antagonism is not universal. Diehards continue to be holdouts from the new team spirit. It is undoubtedly true that violence or unalloyed coercion breaks more lines of communication and leaves a greater deposit of ill will. On the other hand, pure persuasion is probably even more conducive to community, especially under conditions in which the group process operates most creatively. Such persuasive interaction is not sufficiently effective, however, in conflicts involving deep-rooted interests, or requiring rapid, far-reaching change against entrenched monopolies of power. A network of discussion groups cannot even choose a new governor unless they are supplemented by elections that restrain minority parties from office. There is no basic social change without sharp conflict between power groups. This being the case, nonviolent resistance ought to be compared not with utopian impossibilities but with other methods appropriate for gaining difficult social ends. Even though its community-building consequences are somewhat mixed, nonviolent resistance can be said to have a better record than other methods that might be attempted for similar purposes.

Because the method maintains fellowship to a greater degree during the struggle, it also allows a fuller and quicker development of cooperative relationships after the struggle. Since the chasm never becomes as wide as it might, bridges are more easily built across it. General Smuts, Gandhi's direct opponent in South Africa, still contributed a sincerely appreciative essay to a volume that was published honoring Gandhi's seventieth birthday. In it he said, "I must frankly admit that his activities at that time were very trying to me." But he also went on to speak of the spirit of goodwill that persisted through the struggle. "There was no hatred or personal ill feeling, the spirit of humanity was never absent, and when the fight was over there was the atmosphere in which a decent peace could be concluded."[25]

A similar testimony is found in a special report of the Southern Regional Council, a group whose orientation has been toward scholarly research and responsible education. The report commented: "One of the finest of the features of the sit-ins has been an evident invigoration of the bonds of community in the South. . . . The sit-ins have not engendered lingering animosities, but on the contrary have frequently produced a readiness on the part of whites to move on to further stages of desegregation."[26]

Although some opponents would be less tolerant than those just referred to, nonviolent resistance has tended to avoid the buildup of hostility that one might expect in similar tense situations. Resisters have tried to avoid not only violence but also expressions of bitterness. They have not therefore triggered as many resentments and animosities to carry over into the postconflict period. They have to a significant degree avoided the psychological reprisals that tend to follow more vehement attacks.

Reconciling aspects loom larger in the strategies of nonviolence. Although justice outranks it, harmony with the opponent has a high place on the resister's list of priorities. The aim is not so much a unilateral triumph, accompanied by the humiliation of the opponent. The tactics used are intended preferably to create a situation in which negotiation can take place. It is expected that the resulting agreement will, to a considerable extent, be mutually advantageous. Such a double victory will leave less possibility for a triumphant winner rising over a frustrated, vanquished loser, and more possibility for mutual respect and common satisfaction.

Such a degree of difference is possible so long as there are overlapping interests as well as conflicting interests. In terms of game theory, this assumes that to a certain extent, at least, conflicts are not "constant-sum games" (in which the sum of the gains of participants is fixed) but rather "variable-sum games" (in which more for one does not necessarily mean less for the other). The just solution, arrived at with the help of "truth force," should finally bring some gains to both sides, even though they may not be all that either side wanted originally.

Instead of trying to intensify class struggle or intergroup conflict, nonviolent resistance at its best tries to deal with the basic alienation between persons. It approaches this by a deeper awakening of concern, a fuller recognition of the realities of life for the opposite group, and a somewhat greater willing of the good for the opponent. This is not to say that one dominant group or class may not decisively have to give up its prerogatives. Nor is it to say that such a surrender will be made happily and voluntarily. But it is to say that, along with the compulsory and the contractual, which are still necessary in human relationships, it is also possible to incorporate more cooperative ties. An adequate aim is not the mere absence of violence, but also the presence of goodwill. When quarreling children are shut in separate rooms, the family may have quiet but not harmony. Even in conflicts of basic interest, we ought to push as far as possible toward methods that allow more genuine reconciliation.

Such a community of love is the social goal of the Christian faith. Its full meaning for all social groupings we see only through a glass darkly. Yet in the close comradeship of the church we have experienced something of its reality. "For he is our peace, who has made us both one, and has broken down the dividing wall of hostility." (Eph. 2:14.) Through our responsible action in the choice of means, God may yet find openings through which to order affairs justly as well as to reconcile groups compassionately.

6

A REALISTIC VIEW OF THE LIMITATIONS OF NONVIOLENCE

Gandhi's last prayer address before leaving the ashram at Sabarmati for the salt march ended with these words:

I have faith in the righteousness of our cause and the purity of our weapons. And where the means are clean, there God is undoubtedly present with His blessings. And where these three combine, there defeat is an impossibility. A Satyagrahi, whether free or incarcerated, is ever victorious. He is vanquished only when he forsakes truth and non-violence and turns a deaf ear to the Inner Voice. If, therefore, there is such a thing as defeat for even a Satyagrahi, he alone is the cause of it. God bless you all and keep off all obstacles from the path in the struggle that begins tomorrow. Let this be our prayer.[1]

These are words of courage and conviction. Are they also an expression of naïveté? Is it true that there can be no defeat for nonviolent resisters so long as they personally meet the necessary requirements? On another occasion, Gandhi wrote: "Non-violence has no limits. If a particular dose does not seem to answer, more should be administered. It is a never-failing remedy."[2] Would this be true against a ruthless dictator whose mechanized armies took over a country? Could suffering affect troops launching nuclear rockets from a thousand miles away? Would nonviolent direct action be an invincible enforcement strategy for the United Nations? How widely effective can this method be expected to be? How extensive a contribution can it make to a panoply of Christian means toward social ends?

In order to answer such questions, it is helpful to outline the factors that contribute to success or failure in a campaign of nonviolent resistance. Then one may ask to what extent these factors can be expected to be present in a particular situation. This will provide a sounder basis for analyzing the suitability of the method for a variety of circumstances. Predictions of outcome are always hazardous, especially when there are few precedents. Yet in introducing much-needed social inventions, we are always in this situation. We can at least do the best we can with the data we have.

There are three groups of important factors related to the success or failure of nonviolent resistance. More specific observations can be made under the general headings of the nature of the groups involved, the strategies used, and the social environment for the struggle.

One aspect of the nature of the groups is the size of the resisting body and that of their opposition. Study of the social process of nonviolent resistance has suggested that the number who actually undertake resisting action is not as important as might be expected. The more decisive factor is the number and importance of the allies they are able to win. The shift of allegiance of third parties can be effected by comparatively small contingents. Other characteristics of the resisting group and of their direct opponents are more important than their numbers. This is especially true if the primary appeal exerted in a particular struggle is a persuasive one. If, however, resisters rely heavily on coercion even to win support from third parties, then numbers become more important. A boycott can be effective only when a high enough percentage of patrons stay out of a store.

In two respects, an increase in numbers of resisters may actually become a handicap. Violent expressions by resisters are more likely to occur if the group includes many who are not fully committed or trained. Also, the larger the reform group (even potentially), the more fear and anxiety may be generated within both opponents and onlookers. Social change toward equal racial opportunity has tended to be more difficult in communities with a higher percentage of minority group citizens. In such situations, however, there seems to be no acceptable alternative to working through the sharper conflict that is necessarily involved. If gains are to be made at all, they must be made against stronger opposition. This is likely to require more coercion and larger numbers supporting the resistance movement.

An even more important factor is the degree of commitment of the groups involved. Intensity of feeling and conviction is important because it is related to the lengths to which groups are willing to go. How are life situations and priorities of values defined? Is there a deep sense of mission or religious calling? How much are opponents prepared to lose before they will make concessions? How persistent are resisters before the increasing severity of repression? As has been pointed out in a preceding chapter, their initial militancy may consolidate the opposition. Are they able to continue sufficiently longer to begin the process of dividing the opposition through suffering?

Martin Luther King expressed such an intention in these words directed "to our most bitter opponents": "We shall match your capacity to inflict suffering by our capacity to endure suffering. . . . Do to us what you will. . . . But be ye assured that we will wear you down by our capacity to suffer."[3] A leader in the Gandhian movement described the possible meaning of this during an incident of soldiers' firing into a demonstration. He wrote: "When those in front fell down wounded by the shots, those behind came forward with their breasts bared and exposed themselves to the fire, so much so that some people got as many as twenty-one bullet wounds in their bodies and all the people stood their ground without getting into a panic."[4] The depth of the reservoirs of heroism and courage are always important in difficult social change.

Closely related to these personal qualities is the solidarity of the groups involved. Both resisters and their opponents face problems of unity and morale. The opposition group tends to include both diehards and those willing to make some concessions. The problem then is to prevent detachment of support. Among the resisters some are likely to be more militant, whereas others are more moderate. Group cohesion is increased by hostile pressure from outside. Yet it is still a problem for leadership to fuse persons of varying viewpoints into a single movement.

Some in both groups appear to be more ready to resort to violence. Firing into crowds, using fire hoses, or hanging dissenters has not been condoned by all *status quo* groups. Negro juvenile gangs have stoned cars or thrown fire bombs into white stores to the serious embarrassment of nonviolent leaders. Gandhi had to face those who felt that some violence was necessary. One critic felt that "nonviolent revolution" was as contradictory as "vegetarian tiger."[5] Another wrote, "We do not want to develop a nation of women who know only how to suffer and not how to strike."[6] On the other hand, Gandhi had to restrain those who were so enthusiastic about nonviolent campaigns that they wanted to launch them on every conceivable occasion.[7]

Gandhi's religious position constantly threatened erosion for his movement. Extremely orthodox Hindus were frequently discontented and Moslems were often suspicious. Some university students said, "Gandhiji's constant reference to God, truth and non-violence is nauseating; it stinks in our nostrils."[8] Elderly Vedanta philosophers expressed regret about Gandhi's ignorance of spiritual matters and longed to lead him into more advanced stages of enlightenment.[9] It is significant that Riddle, in presenting methods used to maintain loyalty among early Christians, should give his book *The Martyrs* the subtitle "A Study in Social Control." The outcome of nonviolent struggle depends significantly on the ability to hold either side together.

A fourth factor related to the nature of groups is the comparative status of participants. Examples have already been cited that show how a greater appeal is made to the public by persons who hold prestige or possess a reputation for political wisdom or sound social contribution. A cause is more likely to win adherents if its proponents are generally admired. Opposing groups are less likely to see each other as outsiders or strangers if they share common characteristics in matters like education, class, or social grooming. Any preexisting prejudice against a group makes their campaign more difficult. On the other hand, groups or individuals are more likely to succeed if there is already a kindly disposition toward them on grounds different from the issues in the campaign.

Another group of factors in success is related to goals and strategies. These include the magnitude of the change sought. How much threat is involved to existing concepts and structures by demands of the resisters? Goals within a common cultural framework are easier to achieve than those which would shatter the system. If a proposal can be related to established meanings and accepted forms, it gains a note of familiarity and legitimacy. How flexible are campaigners in negotiation? Are they willing to settle for modest gains or do they insist on thorough renovations? The latter may sometimes be necessary, but it is also more difficult. As Lewis A. Coser puts it, on the basis of his study of conflicts in general: "The smaller the sacrifice a party demands from the opponent, the more limited the aims, the higher the chances that the potential loser will be ready to give up battle. The loser must be led to decide that peace is more attractive than the continuation of the conflict; such a decision will be powerfully enhanced if the demands made upon him are not exorbitant."[10]

Severe persecution can be successful only if the idea or movement against which it is directed can be made to seem outrageous in the scope of its demand. On the other hand, the goals of resisters must be sufficiently advanced that they will seem important enough to discontented persons. They must promise sufficient gain to enlist supporters, but not demand so much as to alienate the general population. The issue should be defined in such a way as to attach maximum support to the campaign and to detach maximum support from the opposition. Gandhi, for example, made a masterful play when he selected the salt tax as a target for civil disobedience. It was widely unpopular among the Indians. At the same time, the British were divided on the issue, with many already opposing the tax.

In addition to the goals in any campaign, the strategies or tactics adopted are also an important factor. A decision that must be made by any nonviolent movement is how radical its nonconforming conduct should be. The analysis of the social process of nonviolent resistance has indicated the dilemma of the Satyagrahi. Any resisting group must steer always between the perils of fanaticism on the one hand and of respectability on the other. If tactics are not far enough beyond the customary, the unique strengths of nonviolent resistance are not released. If action is too radical, it is more likely to be successfully repressed. It may be doubted that even in days of more dramatic controversy the reform was aided by the kind of excesses exhibited by a few Quakers in the Massachusetts Bay Colony. Thomas Newhouse broke two glass bottles in a Boston church as a sign "that so they should be dashed to pieces." As a protest Lydia Wardel entered the Newbury church naked. Margaret Brewster appeared in the Old South Church in sackcloth and ashes, with her hair down and face blackened.[11] Such action is exceptional, but it has appeared on the fringes of other nonviolent protest movements. Extremists among conscientious objectors in World War II included one who spent over four hundred days in repeated fasts, who kept delivering impassioned diatribes, and who in prison refused to cooperate at all, even to dressing himself.[12] Short of such radical conduct, there are still some oddities and eccentricities that irritate unnecessarily. As nonessential impediments they had best be dropped by resisters.

Opponents also face an important decision regarding defense strategy. Their dilemma is between ineffectiveness in restraining resisters on the one hand and offending the public on the other. The range of possibilities, from friendly aid to extermination, has already been described. Opponents also face an area of proscribed behavior. Although resisters need to produce martyrs, their antagonists face the necessity of controlling them without making martyrs. Toward this end some tactics are functional, whereas others prove to be dysfunctional.

Both sides also strengthen or weaken their positions by the particular blend of their mixture of persuasion and pressure of other kinds. If it is true that both are usually necessary and that there are often some conflicting consequences, the particular "mix" adopted is important. Expressions of goodwill for persons and denunciation for actions are hard to combine into healing doses. The same is true of the most prudent compounding of coercion or concession. To what extent can gratitude be won by supporting an opponent, or how far is it necessary to compel him by undermining his position? These are troublesome test questions for leadership.

Such questions apply not only to the action and reaction patterns peculiar to nonviolent resistance. They relate also to the supplementary techniques that both sides are likely to use. Propaganda may or may not be convincing. Court cases may be well handled or ill advised. Political action requires skill and imagination if it is to be suitably chosen or effectively managed. Even the most persistent and dedicated of campaigners may be the weaker for poor tactics in these supporting areas.

A last factor related to strategy is the quality and type of leadership involved. The strength of a movement depends to a considerable extent on the competence of its leadership. India was fortunate in Gandhi, and the American people should be appreciative of Martin Luther King. In both of their movements, however, local campaigns sometimes failed because of the lack of ability among subordinate leaders.

The task faced is of heroic proportions. Resistance leaders must handle four fronts: facing toward their direct opponents, the general public, their own resisting group, and onlookers outside the immediate society. Opposition leaders must deal with a comparable set of four groups. Problems of organization in a major campaign are formidable, especially when undertaken in the face of intimidation or suppression. The Indian National Congress established offices down to small villages. Other organizations for supporting purposes were related to it in a complex structure of satellites. In such a movement, problems of relationships, finance, and program are not cared for by general religious idealism alone.

Further study is needed on the comparative effectiveness of different types of leaders. Colonial Quakers and the earliest lunch counter sit-ins seem to have been comparatively unorganized, *laissez-faire* efforts. The Negro protest movement soon developed more democratic forms for policy determination. Within a democratic structure, Gandhi asserted such predominant influence that he has been called dictatorial. His leadership was decidedly charismatic. Miracles were attributed to him. Many people believed in his infallibility. His blessing was thought to be particularly potent. Gandhi believed in democracy, had a high regard for minorities, and on occasion yielded to the advice of other leaders. Yet he could also be harsh to his subordinates. He contended that anyone might withdraw from a Satyagrahi army, but that while persons were participating, all must obey the leader.

Nehru was a loyal and admiring follower. Yet he could also say, in connection with the Patna meeting of the All-India Congress Committee, that Gandhi seemed to be "his old dictatorial self." When Gandhi demanded acceptance of his conditions before he would give leadership, Nehru felt that this "was perfectly natural, for one could not both have him and ask him to act against his own deeply felt convictions. But there seemed too much of imposition from above and too little of mutual discussion and hammering out a policy. It is curious how Gandhiji dominates the mind and then complains of the helplessness of people."[13]

It may be that different circumstances or different leadership positions require more of a democratic or more of a dictatorial approach. Or perhaps nonviolent resistance in this respect lies between a town meeting and an army, requiring stronger leadership than the first and less autocratic command than the second. Or, we may find that here also, as in so many other situations, democratic leadership is a superior form so long as circumstances allow communication and discussion. On this matter, we require more data before venturing a research-based judgment.

Some of the most important factors in the success or failure of nonviolent resistance are found in the general social context. For one thing, the degree of prevailing discontent is important. Are there enough persons seriously wanting change that they will join a nonviolent movement? No major campaign can be launched if no one will follow the leader. A resisting force can be more quickly built where there are deep grievances awaiting articulation. As William Robert Miller puts it, "The masses speak in question marks and exclamation marks, looking for someone to write out the words, which they will then recognize as their own questions and exclamations."[14] The leader first of all must speak for someone. Only then can he suggest strategy or organize a movement.

Another important consideration, emphasized in tracing the typical history of a campaign, is the presence of third parties who may detach their support from repressive authorities. The availability of such potential allies is a major matter in predicting victory for resisters. Is society homogeneously solidified behind the existing situation, or is it sufficiently heterogeneous to allow groups to transfer allegiance? Are there strong liberal groups or persons already unfriendly to the authorities? Do they have available ways for expressing themselves? Is the general population humanitarian enough to be concerned about suffering? Are there influential sources of pressure from outside the community involved in the struggle?

So much depends on this kind of pressure or withdrawal of support that it is doubtful whether any major use of nonviolent resistance could succeed without such third-party help. It is possible to drive a wedge into the group of active opponents, converting part of them into a kind of third party, but it is unlikely that this would often be sufficient. Especially the leaders of the opposition typically need to be coerced. They are much more difficult to convert, since they have made a heavy emotional investment in their previous position. They have placed their views emphatically on public record. Their prestige and power are at stake in any recantation. In the quotation at the beginning of this chapter, Gandhi suggests that the resisters are alone the cause of their own defeat or victory. In this he is surely carried away by his own enthusiasms. The practitioners of any social method are inextricably a part of an interdependent society. It is a mistake to assume that they can succeed without some help found in the general social situation.

In addition to a spectrum of potential group support for the resisters, there are other limiting political or economic circumstances that may restrict opponents. Gandhi on occasion refused to take advantage of a government hard pressed in war. Yet the very existence of such a national emergency made it expedient for government to reduce discontent behind its own lines. Near the middle of the last century, Hungarian resistance to Austria was more likely to succeed because Austria needed Hungarian cooperation in its difficulties with Denmark and Prussia. In 1905 nonviolent resistance in Finland won a restoration of earlier national rights at a time when Russia was being defeated by Japan and the czar was facing insurrection in St. Petersburg. When Russia was again in a more favorable position, it rescinded some of its concessions. During World War II, the Nazis needed as little disorder as possible in Norway and Denmark. If resistance was weak enough, they might feel that a quick and relentless liquidation of objectors would intimidate the population. If this seemed unlikely, however, minor concessions under the circumstances became preferable to diverting still more troops from the fighting fronts. Another type of environmental support for resisters is now being illustrated by the industrial underdevelopment of the southern part of the

United States. The desire to attract northern factories has been one of the factors moderating attitudes toward resisters. Likewise, in Gandhi's campaign the depression of the '30's was an additional economic factor already causing a decline in British exports. This tended to reinforce the effect of the Indian boycott.

A third general social consideration is the compatibility between the demands of resisters and the cultural trends of the times. Is this an idea whose time has come? How obvious does the maladjustment appear to be? Have other nations or regions already made the change? Are there other historical forces that support a trend toward the objectives of the campaign? When positive answers can be given to questions such as these, the goal of a resisting group more easily commends itself as truth. Persons observing the suffering of resisters are more likely to reconsider their own position if that position has already been called into question by other developments.

One indication of readiness for social change may be the strength of moderate reform groups whose aims are similar to those of the more militant resisters. Such groups use different tactics. When President Wilson visited Boston in February, 1919, the more conventional suffragists presented him with a bouquet of jonquils. The militants picketed his reviewing stand.[15] Moderate and militant wings of a reform movement may have little patience with each other. Picketing suffragists were reported to refer to the more conservative reformers as "old fogies and perfect ladies." A leader of the moderates, on the other hand, spoke of the militant wing as "the I.W.W. of the suffrage movement."[16] Yet the two groups normally supplement each other. In difficult types of change, both are probably necessary. Moderate reform groups not only reflect the degree of readiness for change, but they also help to form a supportive climate of opinion for the ends of nonviolent resisters.

Apart from various groups of reformers, there are even more important indications of parallel cultural trends. Successful instances of nonviolent resistance are mere episodes in more sweeping movements of historical change. As women began increasingly to work outside the home, it became more likely that they would be granted the right to vote. Religious liberty became easier to win when general expressions of tolerance became more prominent in literature and political agitation. As theologies grew less dogmatic, religious authorities became more merciful. A changing cultural climate regarding imperialism or race relations has aided nonviolent resisters in those fields. This is a reciprocal relationship. Nonviolent resistance contributes to a changing social climate. At the same time it is supported by whatever favorable changes have previously taken place. A resistance campaign must move far enough ahead of the *status quo* to accelerate progress. It can also the more easily do this if it is moving in the same direction as other important elements in existing culture.

All the above elements in effective resistance are related to two major critical factors in the power relationships of the groups involved. With regard to resisters and their direct opponents, the decisive point is their comparative capacities for enduring suffering and effecting repression. If resisters are able to endure more punishment than their opponents are free to direct toward them, the campaign is likely to achieve some success. This is related to a second central issue, one that involves third parties. The outcome depends also on the comparative abilities of resisters and opponents by either persuasion or coercion to detach support from each other under prevailing historical circumstances. All the factors related to the nature of the two groups, goals and strategies, and the general social situation, come to a focus at this point. Opponents are placed in an especially hopeless position if the unorthodox conduct of the resisters is either the practice of the end sought or publicity so convincing that it will eventually win the public even though resisters are not made to suffer. If such conduct is not opposed, the resisters achieve their goal. If suppression is attempted and widespread popular sympathy for the resisters results, the nonconformists also win. When sufficiently persistent resisters use nonviolent tactics so capable of detaching support under prevailing cultural conditions, opponents cannot then allow the unorthodox conduct to continue, nor can they attempt to stop it, without victory for the resisters.

Previous chapters have included abundant historical evidence of such potential power in nonviolent resistance. It has proved to be effective when violent means were unavailable or would have been crushed or would have resulted in such losses as far to outweigh any gains. It has also successfully supplemented more conventional forms of persuasion where they alone would have been inadequate. In situations involving surrender of basic power or privilege, for example, nonviolent resistance adds a supplementary strength to more customary means. Especially during an era in which more rapid social change is required, there may be a wider range of uses for the method than we have ordinarily thought.

This is comparatively clear with respect to difficult types of domestic reform in a democracy. Just as the method has filled a unique need in race relations, it might also do so in types of industrial disputes or in general social change. Nonviolence may become necessary in our search for equality of economic opportunity, which will still remain to be won even after racial segregation has disappeared. Nonviolent resistance presents itself as a strategy for the unemployed, the poor, and their allies among social liberals, should opposition to their just demands prove to be stubborn.

Also some types of international action can apparently be well accomplished through nonviolent resistance. It should never be forgotten that Gandhi's campaign was in effect international, being directed against those who determined policy in England. Under similar conditions other colonial rebellions might be accomplished by nonviolent resistance.

We can speak with greater assurance about such uses of the method. In these areas the essential factors contributing to success may more clearly become available. There is impressive historical experience to support the claim not only that nonviolent resistance is morally superior to violence and grosser forms of coercion, but that it can also be socially effective under circumstances as described. It is not necessary to discuss this at greater length here, since previous chapters have already dealt with this in some detail.

At this point it is interesting to speculate about possible extensions of the method. Some areas seem to have considerable similarity to those in which resistance has already been successfully attempted. For one thing, might nonviolent resistance be used as a method of social control as well as a method of social change? Could it occasionally become a form of citizen support of police action, in order to protect legislative or social gains already made? Gandhi was convinced, for example, that a peace brigade could quell riots by standing between the two fighting groups and receiving their blows. This suggests problems in logistic placement! It may be, however, that there is a domestic counterpart to the presence of the United Nations, which has proved reasonably effective in some trouble spots of the world. Or, in addition to whatever police and courts may do, nonviolent demonstrations might further mobilize public opinion against those who were circumventing or violating laws, let us say against child labor or racial discrimination.

Conceivably this might be developed into an additional method for enforcing world law or standards for human rights under an international organization such as the United Nations. Should the principle of policed international controls come to be more fully accepted, nonviolent forces from abroad might join the resistance against some entrenched evil within a country, as for example apartheid in South Africa. Dramatic expressions of the intensity of world feeling might be peculiarly potent against nations concerned about preserving their international image in the eyes of other countries. Especially within democracies, support of larger sections of the citizenry might also be secured in this way rather than by other more threatening measures.

There are three major situations that present even greater difficulties, however. They are the most troublesome challenge

to any method of social change in our time. Arriving at a realistic view concerning the usefulness of nonviolent resistance
here becomes an even more speculative matter. We would like
to have a great deal more evidence than is available. Yet the
problems are important enough that we need to do the best
we can with the knowledge we have. These "big three" questions are: (1) Can nonviolent resistance be used against modern
military weapons, especially when fired at long range? (2) Might
nonviolent resistance be a defense against external aggression,
a substitute for war in the case of full-scale military invasion?
(3) Could nonviolent resistance be successfully used as a method
of revolution against totalitarian dictators?[17]

The first of these problems, the use of nonviolence against
long-range weapons, is intensified by modern military technology. Warfare has been mechanized. Rockets strike thousands
of miles from their launching sites. The persons who press the
buttons to send the rockets on their way do not see the destruction that results. They have no personal contact with their
victims. Even under such circumstances, Gandhi was convinced that his method could work. When asked how he would
use nonviolence against the atomic bomb, he replied: "I would
meet it by prayerful action. . . . I would come out in the open
and let the pilot see that I had not the face of evil against him.
The pilot would not see my face at such a height, I know. But
the longing in our heart that he will not come to harm will
reach up to him and his eyes would be opened."[18]

Even as early as 1937, an American supporter of Gandhi took
a different position. Impressed by the depersonalization of warfare that had already taken place by that date, Devere Allen
wrote, "The kindling eye, the Christ-like glance, the flaming
word of unconquerable goodwill, cannot, alas, reach up from
kindled homes and flaming cities to the aviator, thousands of
feet above, who hurls down with mechanical precision his
incendiary burden on persons he has never seen, whose names
he does not know, and whose institutions he has been taught by
clever propaganda to abhor."[19]

Most of us would justifiably vote for the Devere Allen version of these two parallel quotations. So far as direct influence on opponents is concerned, the problem here is accessibility to communication. One cannot offer full nonviolent resistance directly toward a distant bombardier any more than one could toward the inhabitants of a distant planet if they should now begin showering a stream of bombs on the earth.

There are a few things, however, to be said on the other side of the issue. Earthly attackers, even at an immense distance, are partly accessible. Limited or indirect communication may be accomplished. Although we cannot communicate by conversation or, so far as we now know, by "the longing in our heart," we would convey something by nonretaliation. If we possessed the capability of striking back, but chose not to develop or to use that capability, policy makers in the attacking country would know that they were killing us, but that their own country was not being bombed. In other words, they would knowingly be decimating a people at peace. It is debatable whether under such circumstances they would continue their exercise in barbarism. Insofar as their own citizens or other nations possessed this knowledge, they might withdraw their support or bring influence to bear to stop the aggression. An extremely truncated form of the process of nonviolent resistance might then have taken place.

It might be expected that any attacker opposed by nonviolence would soon shift from bombing to invasion. Normally it would appear to be in the aggressor's economic, political, and military interest to occupy a country as intact as possible. If invasion took place, personal contact would become feasible and more classical forms of nonviolent resistance might be attempted, with such possible results as will be considered below in this chapter.

While bombs are actually falling, however, little can be done by traditional nonviolent techniques. Satyagraha has only limited relevance once a full-scale nuclear attack has started. It is small comfort to observe that all-out nuclear retaliation then also has little relevance to righteous outcomes. There are some social situations so deteriorated that there is no way of reversing the course of tragedy. This is still a moral universe, in which evil has consequences. The most important observation to make about the relationship of nonviolent direct action to modern military technology is that insights derived from the resistance process may be used to prevent the outbreak of nuclear holocaust. Some such implications of suffering love for general social policy will be considered in the next chapter.

A second extraordinarily difficult assignment for nonviolent resistance would be its use against a major military invasion. What could be done against an occupying army? Some have suggested that a nonviolent corps might stand in the path of the aggressor, forcing him either to desist or ruthlessly to run over the resisters. It is true that United Nations observers in some turbulent areas have helped keep the peace where it was in the national interests of possible aggressors to avoid international complications. Presumably, however, a peace-keeping contingent drawn solely from the threatened country would have less influence, especially if the aggressor's national interests strongly favored invasion. Furthermore, modern invasion routes being what they are, defensive forces would seem to face an almost impossible problem in making initial contact. Even a nonviolent assemblage at all airports could not confront parachutists in the back country.

More realistic is the standard strategy most frequently proposed by proponents of nonviolence. This would allow invaders to occupy a country, but would then refuse to cooperate with them. Orders would be ignored. Homes and factories would not be voluntarily surrendered. If an attempt was made to operate factories, workers would go on strike. Citizens would prefer death to submission. In addition to disobeying official commands of the alien troops, there has been some disagreement as to whether they should also be personally ostracized, or whether they should be met with kindness, thus establishing closer bonds of sympathy.

Any such major noncooperation would result in casualties and suffering. These very losses, by the alchemy of nonviolent resistance, might be transmuted into genuine gains. Portions

of the occupying army might be won over by the sight of masses
of human beings willing to be killed rather than obey. Experience and further research might show that this is an even
greater possibility if kindness is shown to the occupiers as individual persons. There would also be less readiness to liquidate
a population since the invaders would not first have fought a
war to break into the country and would not have built up the
animosities resulting from hostilities. Stephen King-Hall, writing from a military background, has observed: "The distinction
between an occupation as the climax of a military battle and
one as the beginning of a psychological struggle is of the utmost
importance. It is the difference between the argument of force
and the force of an argument."[20]

In response to sympathy and their own interests, other countries could be led to apply sanctions of various kinds to the
invading nation, or at least the aggressor would damage its
international appeal as a peaceful nation. In the contemporary
contest for influence in nonaligned areas, this could become an
important consideration. It is also conceivable that the population of the attacking nation would detach its support from a
policy involving brutality, loss of prestige, and economic waste.
So long as resistance continued, few rewards would be reaped
by the invader in the form of trade, military support, commercial profits, or spread of ideas. At the same time, heavy costs
would have to be underwritten by taxpayers for maintaining
larger occupying forces abroad than would be necessary with a
supine population. This might become an especially effective
consideration if it were possible for the invaded country to
promise that after the withdrawal of troops concessions would
be made in a mutually acceptable accommodation.

It is possible that such resistance to invasion might present
the opponent with the kind of dilemma created by successful
nonviolent action. If substantially the entire population refused to cooperate, the invader could not compel obedience
without destroying the labor force he needed to serve his ends.
If no one obeyed, he could not rule. By increasing penalties, he

would defeat his own regime in the process of trying to stamp out opposition to his regime. Forms of nonviolent resistance have had a limited success historically against invasion, as in the general strike against the 1920 Kapp putsch in Germany or the opposition of some professional groups to Nazi control in Norway. To a certain extent the Gandhi movement is an illustration. Although it was not a defense against full-scale war, it did involve opposition to a foreign regime buttressed by military power. Depending on the character of the invading nation and the general world situation, nonviolent resistance might be successful in even more serious modern instances of invasion. Theoretically all the major factors in the success of nonviolent resistance could be present.

The chief practical problem, however, would seem to lie at the point of the persistence and solidarity of the resisters. Under these circumstances a very great deal would be required of the invaded population. Only in the most unusual situations would there seem to be a basis for the deep and united opposition necessary to continuing high morale. Not only would men have to accept severe punishment from invaders but long-continued refusal to work would lead to their own starvation. How long would parents be willing to see their children go without food before they would either resort to sabotage and violence, or begin to cooperate with the enemy? To avoid famine, a population might continue economic production and confine disobedience to other selected regulations promulgated by the invader. It is hard to see how this would be enough to force withdrawal, since the invader could make a few concessions and still reap continuous economic gains.

For successful resistance it would appear as though almost the entire population would need to be thoroughly committed to nonviolence to the death. If a substantial segment gave up resistance, the invader could see reason to remain. Against weapons trained on a country from a distance, the average citizen can do nothing but absorb the attack. Against an invading force the individual citizen can do something else. He can collaborate. We dare not underestimate the power of fear and terror to compel compliance. There is also counterpower latent in men that can be energized by God. The problem is whether the generality of men are sufficiently open to God's leading. A response of such heroic proportions would certainly require a great deal of advance preparation, including a striking maturing of the spiritual resources of a nation. It is doubtful whether the kinds of training envisaged by pacifists would be sufficient under existing international circumstances.

It may well be, however, that in the future this will become a genuine possibility, even as it becomes a more evident necessity. When a basic social change has been accomplished, what was previously utopian becomes attainable. The change creates its own problems, and finite man is still limited by ambiguous situations. Yet he is now dealing with a new order of problems. Once the popular mind-set toward slavery or the position of women was altered, it became feasible to deal with issues and proposals previously thought ludicrous. Now we see as live options positions of privilege and leadership for both racial minorities and women that once would not even have been seriously discussed. So also, as a population's general orientation toward violence changes, a new range of alternatives opens up. As weapons become more destructive, we may as thoroughly reject full-scale violence as we have rejected slavery. Under such circumstances one would expect a more universal readiness to accept novel ways and to define socially sanctioned heroism in nonviolent terms. It might well then become more normal to invest energy in the spiritual growth prerequisite to nonviolent resistance against major invasion.

The most difficult situation in which nonviolent resistance might be attempted is against a ruthlessly violent dictatorship after it has become solidly established in power. Such totalitarianism might be faced from a colonial area or an invaded country, or from within the dictatorship itself.

Gandhi's faith did not falter even before this problem. Believing that nonviolence is the most efficacious in the face of the greatest violence, he confidently asserted: "Even a heart of flint will melt in front of a fire kindled by the power of soul. Even a Nero becomes a lamb when he faces love."[21] He was willing to apply this in modern times also. He claimed: "Even if Hitler was so minded, he could not devastate seven hundred thousand nonviolent villages. He would himself become nonviolent in the process."[22] In reply to the argument that Hitler and Mussolini were incapable of moral response, Gandhi said: "Your argument presupposes that dictators like Mussolini or Hitler are beyond redemption. But belief in nonviolence is based on the assumption that human nature in its essence is one and therefore unfailingly responds to the advances of love." If Hitler and Mussolini were met with nonviolence, he continues, "it is not only highly likely, but I hold it to be inevitable, that they would recognize the superiority of nonviolent resistance over any display of violence that they may be capable of putting forth." Besides, according to Gandhi, nonviolent techniques do not depend on the goodwill of dictators, but on "the unfailing assistance of God." A resister's faith in this "makes him indomitable."[23]

Gandhi was right in his awareness of God's help and man's general potentiality. He was wrong in overlooking that human nature is not "one" in its response to God and in its realization of the divine potentiality within. He underestimated the pervasiveness of sin and the depth of the rebellion that is also possible for man. The British as opponents were decidedly different than the Nazis would have been. Although civil rights were infringed upon, nevertheless Gandhi reaped the advantage of considerable freedom of speech, not only in India, but for news reports and public discussion in Great Britain and in other countries of the world. He faced leaders who were comparatively humanitarian and who were often liberal in general social outlook. The Amritsar massacre in India was not the same as Buchenwald or Bergen-Belsen in Germany, nor was it as often repeated.

The illustrations that are cited of successful nonviolent resistance against dictatorship often do not involve the problem at its worst. The remarkable rescue of Jews from Denmark was an evacuation operation in a geographical location fortunately near Sweden. It was not significantly, and certainly not successfully, a struggle for change in the policy of the regime. The Norwegian resistance movement demonstrated great nobility and some success. Further study of its history should prove extremely fruitful. Even so, it occurred while the German Nazi dictatorship was fighting a war for its life. Deliverance finally came through military victory for the allies. Again this was not dictatorship in its most difficult manifestation.

Under sufficiently favorable circumstances, as when dictatorship has weaker support, less resolute leadership, or external limitations, the usual forms of nonviolent resistance may have some effect. Persons in an autocratic society still differ in their reaction to suffering. Even totalitarian rulers must depend partly on consent. There may be influential reactions from other countries. In the more serious manifestations of dictatorship, however, several of the key factors in the success of classic nonviolent resistance are likely to be lacking.

In modern dictatorships ruthlessness can be organized with technological efficiency. Suffering may be inflicted to such a degree that the resistance collapses. Protest leadership may be removed into sudden and permanent oblivion. There may be no more qualms about liquidating millions of protesters than there were about wiping out the Jews. When brutality is automated and liquidation mechanized, bureaucrats at the top can order masses to death as though they were statistical compilations. They substitute paper work for what might be impossible for them, the steady killing of one man after another. Intermediates in the chain of command can shift responsibility to their superiors. Those at the actual work face, manning the gas ovens, can be coerced and rotated.

As brutal dictators become firmly established, it becomes unlikely that a mass resistance movement can be put together, or that enough resisters can be trained. The blood of the martyrs historically has not always been the seed of a church. Ideas may live to bear fruit later in a different climate, but in particular situations persecution has been pushed to the point of exterminating sects. Modern dictators are aware of the germinating power of martyr blood and have taken steps to safeguard against it.

The less the opponent and his supporters share the moral presuppositions of the resisting group, the less effective can nonviolent resistance be expected to be. The method will be most easily successful when opponents regard the suffering of resisters as unfortunate and consider the demands of resisters as not too serious a threat. The greater the overlap in the value systems of the groups involved, the sooner one would expect agreement. In our culture we do not generally consider it funny to kick a Jew in the stomach. We tend to feel genuine sympathy for those who are persecuted. A dictatorship may reflect a much different culture. It may glorify violence, by which it gained power, and domination, which it continues to assert. It may consider belligerency and the infliction of pain on inferiors to be morally desirable. Obedience to authority is likely to be regarded as unquestionably good. Nonviolence may be labeled as contemptible weakness. Accepting suffering or resisting the state becomes despicable. Under such a style of life the dictator's severity of repression may feed on the action of resisters, rather than be modified by it.

Nonviolent resistance requires a certain degree of moral development not only among resisters but also among opponents, or at least among the rest of the population. Any improved social procedure must rest to a great extent on a population spiritually able to sustain it. There is a necessary level of moral and social development before democracy becomes possible—or economic cooperation, or international organization, or nonviolent resistance. Where this is lacking there is really no practical alternative to the cruder methods of more paleolithic days, even though the weapons used be those of a nuclear era.

A dictatorship, in addition, has available facilities for censoring suffering. Much of the impact of nonviolent resisters depends upon publicity for their own demonstrations and for the counteraction used against them. Dictators, who have a monopoly of the usual mass communication media, can black out the news or interpret it as best fits their purposes. To a great extent the public can thus be insulated from contact with the arguments and the suffering of protesters.

Complete concealment is unlikely. Even the most rigid secrecy could scarcely hide persecution from the family and immediate friends of the sufferer. Underground movements have improvised networks of communication. Dictators probably would not want a total veiling of their deeds. Punishment becomes a sanction to prevent undesired conduct only if subjects are aware of it. If penalties were completely concealed, they might not arouse sympathy for the punished, but neither would they deter others.

In 1941 before Berggrav was arrested, Himmler is said to have spoken with him, saying: "We'll do it another way. We'll make the people forget you. We don't like to make martyrs, but we have means to make people forget." The bishop's brief reply was, "Try." In this case the bishop's house arrest became an eloquent symbol of resistance. Yet it must also be admitted that dictatorships do possess even more unscrupulous means which are not available in more humane or open societies.

These include not only concealing some facts, but also trumpeting other interpretations by massive propaganda. Psychological manipulation may include brainwashing devices and be reinforced by intensely clever espionage and subversion. It has been suggested that if the Roman emperors had had the resources of modern secret police at their disposal, they would have had some Christians confessing vile intentions to slaughter babies and to set fire to Rome. This can be exaggerated. The church would also have produced some who were persistently loyal to their faith. Yet when we honestly admit how much Christians today are deformed even in democratic societies by propaganda and by pressures to conformity, we will not be too sanguine about resistance to the full psychological armament of modern dictatorship.

One of the major factors in the success of nonviolent resistance has been shown to be the availability of third parties who may detach their support from repressive policies. Such potential allies would also tend to be eliminated in an efficiently ruthless totalitarianism. This could be done not only within a monolithic party or in the home country under dictatorial control. It could also be accomplished in the international expansion of an aggressor nation. Suppose that such a nation, by a kind of salami technique, sliced off one territory after another, taking time in each case firmly to establish its dominance. Finally there would be only two great powers left in the world. If the dictatorship then occupied the other, there would be no independent countries left to bring pressure in support of a nonviolent defense.

To be sure, even dictatorial situations are not entirely so hopeless. The prospect has here been painted at its worst. No dictatorship is completely homogeneous. There is some spark of potential good in every man. Although a much greater devotion and sacrifice would be required against firmly entrenched opponents, a military victory would also be more difficult or even impossible. Yet after all these qualifications are made, it is still true that prospects for successful nonviolent resistance are much dimmer under these circumstances than Gandhi, for example, claimed. Insofar as the contest is one of coercion, dictators possess more effective weapons. Insofar as the decisive element is persuasive, resisters are still severely handicapped. It is not a question of whether the usual forms of nonviolent resistance could ever defeat a dictator. Under favorable conditions this might be done. This would still not be sufficient reason to adopt the method as national policy against all aggressors or all governments. One ought never to argue from a unique instance to a broad generalization.

Under some extremely unfavorable circumstances there is

little or nothing that can be done toward some goals. There are hopeless causes in which for the time being neither violence nor nonviolence can win. We often cannot make up for what we did not do in the past. If we dawdle too much during the first half of our trip to the airport, there is nothing we can do during the second half to get us there on time. Deathbed politics is notoriously difficult. The smaller states of western Europe just before the outbreak of World War II tried desperately but ineffectually to mediate between the two antagonists. There finally was no alternative to Nazi invasion. Imperialists have sometimes delayed the transformation of their colonies into educated, independent, democratic countries until after serious extremist pressure has built up for their delayed emancipation. Then there is no longer any solution that will allow orderly, moderate government. Either the imperialist nation holds power by force, or an extremist revolution wins, or a hurried grant of independence is made to a nation not ready to exercise it. In any of these cases a disorderly, dictatorial, and unstable government is inevitable. Chickens have the habit of coming home to roost. The wages of sin are still death. Time once spent does not return to be reinvested. Unless calamities like ruthless dictatorships have been prevented, there is no immediate option except to live with them. Any hope must be of an extremely long-range sort, linked to vast patience. If God shows such patience in the face of the continuous rebellion of man, and if he continues to live with the consequences of the rebellion, we can expect to do no better. In a world ordered by God's wisdom, there is no other way out except by way of the social consequences of man's apathy and folly.

This does not deliver us from the obligation to act constructively and to do the best possible even under the worst dictatorship. But it does change the character of responsible action. When nonviolent resistance in its usual forms would be inadequate, it ought not to be attempted. Doing the best that can be done is still the calling of God. It is immoral to resort to nonviolent resistance when social conditions guarantee serious losses and defeat. A campaign under such conditions may actually set back the attainment of justice. On the other hand, better methods are not discovered without adventurous experimentation even when there is no full assurance of success.

At least some modification in classical nonviolent resistance would be required under brutal dictatorship. It would seem, for example, that the open truthfulness of the method could not be maintained. Secrecy would become inevitable in the use of an underground press, communications network, or escape routes (as for persecuted Jews). In the French resistance against Nazi persecution, as saintly and dedicated a pacifist as André Trocme found it necessary to support the use of false identification papers. He wrote afterward: "It seemed to us preferable to violate a formal moral rule (absolute truth) in order to apply a living moral rule (the absolute value of the human person). Jesus preferred to violate the Sabbath in order to help the men of his day."[24] Gene Sharp suggests that nonviolence might be organized secretly and practiced openly, as in Norway.[25]

Another modification might theoretically be made in the purpose of resistance. The one slim possibility for rapid modification in a stern dictatorship lies in defection of the armed forces. If by a swift *coup d'état* one section of the army were to seize control, a somewhat more liberal regime might follow. Conceivably, nonviolent resistance might be directed toward producing this kind of split in the military. Success would require a rare combination of circumstances. Any such venture would carry its own hazards of failure or civil war. Surely if nonviolence were directed toward encouraging armed revolution, this would be one of the strangest collections of bedfellows in political history! Yet the underground in totalitarian lands has produced equally strange allies.

Usually, however, action against well-established, ruthless dictatorship would seem to involve an even deeper modification in method. When both violence and the usual forms of nonviolent resistance have become impossible, domestic opponents of a regime very much need a new approach to revolution. Such an approach may be found in the concept of pressure without threat. Under such circumstances the task of the revolutionary becomes a double one. First, he must maintain some manifestation of discontent as a pressure against objectionable features of government. Second, he must not threaten the continued existence of the regime, since that would lead to the liquidation of his protest.

This requires that objecting groups cooperate with existing rulers as far as possible. They might well support programs when their ends and methods are generally acceptable even though their sponsorship is not. One might work in a hospital, for example, as the only means for aiding the sick, even though an objectionable government was paying the bills. From a Christian standpoint this could be regarded as the "best possible" action in a situation very thoroughly saturated with evil. When not everything can be accomplished, at least something can be done. There is some research evidence that in almost impossible situations of sharp disagreement more can be gained in the long run if a person respects the power position of his opponent and avoids destroying his basic power resources. If a person makes it clear that he does not intend to exterminate his antagonist, he may also find that a more secure opponent can more easily afford to listen to grievances and to cooperate with requests.[26]

Within this matrix of general cooperation with the regime it may well be possible to gain slight modifications in policy. Expressions of discontent then come in a real sense from "insiders," those who have won some influence among the supporters of a regime, even though they continue to live in some tension with it. This involves narrowing the range of immediate objectives to minor concessions rather than major reconstruction. As Johannes Hamel put it, in discussing the relationship of the church to dictatorship, "Time and again God creates loopholes, so to speak, open space in the midst of closed systems of unbelief and hatred of God."[27] More limited aims, centering on the "loopholes," are more likely to be won, especially where there is an overlap of interests between objector and ruler. For example, a request to reopen a particular church for a limited range of program activities may seem, even to an antireligious government, to be a way of cementing the loyalty of an important section of the population and yet not allowing those aspects of church program which are most objectionable to the authorities. It would be the hope of the objectors that there would be an accumulation of such slow, small shifts in policy, and that these would eventually add up to major modifications in the regime. Those exerting this kind of limited pressure might not see satisfying results in a single lifetime, but they might well feel that under their extremely difficult circumstances they were contributing all that they possibly could to the future.

The limited creativity possible amid diabolical manifestations of evil tends to be reinforced by a kind of "truth force" in the long processes of history. God not only allows men to rebel and sustains the consequences of their rebellion. He not only continues his initiative wherever men are even partially open to his leading. He has also fixed in creation certain characteristics and sequences in man and nature. If men desire even similar general goals of social welfare, they tend to be led toward those social forms which, under the given conditions of a particular time, best contribute to those ends. Resistance to dictatorship in the long run is supported by those economic and social forces which have moved toward democracy in the past. The requirements of modern technology, the fundamental nature of man, the consequences of public education, all press in the direction of freedom in community. Those within totalitarian societies who desire change are forced to depend more on long historical development and less on immediate campaigns.

Such a strategy of change does not eliminate suffering or martyrdom. Citizens may misjudge governmental reaction to a particular request or type of pressure. Instead of being received as constructive critics, they may be treated as violent enemies. Furthermore, conscientious groups will need to refuse utterly unacceptable forms of cooperation. Equally sincere individuals may differ about where to draw that line. One of the most poignant illustrations of this was the conversation in which Gandhi tried to convince Kagawa that he ought to denounce the Japanese militaristic government even though it meant death for himself and great harm to his cooperatives. Kagawa could not agree, since he was so deeply impressed by the human needs that were being met by the various projects he was engaged in.

There have been equally painful confrontations between Western churchmen and Hromadka in Czechoslovakia or between Christian leaders in Communist China. Yet all would agree that some actions should be unanimously rejected, as, for example, operating the gas chambers in an extermination camp. Some regimes may be so clearly demonic that cooperation is possible at no point at all. Even though there appear to be no positive social consequences to one's refusal, one must then nevertheless act in faith. When there seems to be no way out of a social disaster, one can at least preserve a measure of personal integrity and a short-lived witness to another way of life. At the same time that one may not discern the slightest ray of light in the dark mystery of the future, neither can he foretell the consequences of the tiniest spark struck in the present.

All this underscores the weaknesses of the usual forms of nonviolent resistance against ruthless dictatorships firmly established in power. Yet careful scrutiny of the realistic possibilities leads to an intriguing discovery. Particularly where some measure of cooperation plus minimal pressure is possible, the new strategy of slow change which has been sketched as the only constructive alternative actually turns out to be nonviolent resistance in a modified, severely restricted form. Gandhi would disown it. Other more utopian proponents of nonviolent direct action would oppose it. They are right in insisting that the action involved is considerably different from the classic examples of nonviolent resistance. Acquiescence to the adversary is more complete. Less pressure is exerted. This is not a campaign pushed so far that masses are severely punished.

Yet in its basic characteristics this strategy still preserves the essence of nonviolent resistance. It still involves a degree of nonconformity in doing what is considered to be right, along with a willingness to accept the consequences. Under a rigid dictatorship even slightly unconventional conduct is punished. The area of tolerated behavior is severely contracted, and deviating conduct soon becomes proscribed behavior. Nonviolent resisters characteristically adapt their method to the situation. Severe dictatorship constitutes a greatly altered situation, and therefore requires a greater adaptation. The only method of opposition that holds any significant promise for objectors within the country is nonviolent resistance in a revised version.

7

SUFFERING LOVE AS SOCIAL STRATEGY

In the "latter days," when all peoples shall flow into the house of the Lord and all nations "shall beat their swords into plowshares," Micah felt that God was saying, "The lame I will make the remnant; and those who were cast off, a strong nation" (Micah 4:7). A similar reversal of power coefficients is suggested by Paul's words: "The word of the cross is folly to those who are perishing, but to us who are being saved it is the power of God. . . . The foolishness of God is wiser than men, and the weakness of God is stronger than men. . . . God chose what is foolish in the world to shame the wise, God chose what is weak in the world to shame the strong" (I Cor. 1:18, 25, 27). This is the same inversion of the dominant and the submissive which Jesus described as the meek inheriting the earth (Matt. 5:5). In the Kingdom of God, gain is the by-product of giving, victory may come by concession, and conquest is a consequence of suffering love.

Neither individuals nor groups are yet living in the full quality of relationships that characterize the Kingdom of God. Nations have not yet said, "Come, let us go up to the mountain of the Lord, to the house of the God of Jacob; that he may teach us his ways and we may walk in his paths" (Micah 4:2). We are still occupying the foothills where the air is less pure and visibility is still clouded by the smoggy refuse of imperfect civilization. Those who work for social change are not saintly enough to demonstrate the full power of love. Those who resist change are still devilish enough that they do not always respond to suffering, nor do they invariably recognize a righteous cause.

If suddenly we chanced on a method that won over intransigent opposition without killing a single enemy, that ennobled both sides to the conflict, that reconciled antagonists in deeper bonds of fellowship, and that placed a premium on right instead of might, we ought certainly to adopt that method as a replacement for all previous strategies. These are the values claimed for nonviolent resistance. Yet the method does not completely deliver on its promise. It does cause social turbulence and individual suffering. It is partially a coercive appeal to might. It deepens the resistance of some of its adversaries. Like other methods, it too stands almost helpless before predominantly hopeless circumstances. It provides no magical escape route from the tragedies and ambiguities of the human situation.

Some of these limitations constitute part of the strength of nonviolent resistance within the realities of the existing social climate. Since men are not completely creatures of reason, an unanswerable logical case openly presented is not sufficient grounds for inevitable adoption. Not all persons are sensitive and sympathetic in emotional response; therefore voluntary suffering is not universally moving. Because privileged groups find it easy to disregard most disturbing requests, only those are likely to be heeded which are insistently and powerfully demanded. Nonviolent resistance, by mixing the rational and the emotional, the persuasive and the coercive, becomes more socially effective.

A realistic evaluation of nonviolent resistance tends to magnify its current importance. Recognizing it as less pure than is often claimed makes it also less utopian. Admitting that modifications in the method must be made when strong opposition is being faced makes the general approach more relevant to a wider range of unfavorable circumstances. In the discussion of a realistic ethics of power in an earlier chapter, it was pointed out that social means are arranged along a continuum of in-

creasing compromise, but that one ought to move down the list
only as much as is necessary. The ultimate norm of love is to be
approximated as closely as possible, given the drag of limiting
conditions. In more situations than we commonly expect, nonviolent resistance becomes the best possible action, the strategy
that ought to be adopted by men of goodwill in their struggle
for justice. Although the method can accomplish less than its
more utopian advocates claim, it can do a great deal more than
the general public suspects.

Of course, nonviolence is not a panacea. Even under more
favorable circumstances, those who practice it will not win
every battle, or even every campaign. There still is no substitute
for capable leadership, astute timing, or thorough training.
Resorting to resistance too often on trivial matters would probably lead to diminishing returns. Furthermore, there are limitations to the effectiveness of nonviolent resistance in extremely
difficult situations.

Such a listing of qualifications still leaves the method an
extremely important option. Under the worst of circumstances,
other methods also face grave difficulties. Nonviolence is still
often the most promising among the few strategies available.
Therefore, the most hardheaded of the realists, eager to be
ready for any eventuality, should be more interested in preparing populations to resist nonviolently. Insofar as the training
they provided would include only expedient externalities
rather than the inner spirit of nonviolence, the full impact of
resistance would be blunted. Nevertheless, even military leaders
might accept the method as a possible policy for resisting invasion after violence has failed, for organizing revolution within
the territory or the colonies of a hostile power, or for unseating
a dictator in our desire to expand the free world.[1] George
Kennan once proposed that troops in western Europe be trained
both for offering military defense and for becoming the core
of a civil resistance movement in any territory overrun by the
enemy.[2] Captain B. H. Liddell Hart, a British military strategist,
in commenting on Commander King-Hall's passive resistance

proposals, said, "Even on practical grounds there is a stronger case for nonviolence than is generally realized."[3]

Short of such difficult extremities, there are many more promising situations into which nonviolent resistance can introduce a new power. It provides a less primitive substitute for violence and a more advanced supplement to more conventional methods of reform. It offers an added impetus when change needs to be accelerated or when deep power interests are involved. This is not to say that absolute love has been embodied in community strategy. It is to say that in finite human situations, the best possible approximations to love are also the most realistic social methods.

Nonviolent resistance makes possible a unique blend of characteristics. This is a formula not for a more explosive bomb, but for a more effective peaceful force. The novelty of the protest both dramatizes injustice and presents neglected data in ways that more easily break through selective attention or biased interpretation. Guilt feelings are activated within the opponent, but under circumstances that make it more likely that they will be faced constructively and not be projected on their antagonists. The resistance recipe mixes a large measure of demands with a generous sprinkling of understanding and goodwill. Insofar as they practice self-purification, resisters compound an admission of their own faults with a condemnation of evil in the social situation. They try to seek justice both for their own group and for their opponents. To a considerable extent their methods take suffering on themselves instead of inflicting it on others. In all these respects, Satyagraha is disarming. Opponents have less to fear, especially at the point of threat to personality.

Nonviolent resistance aims to gain emotional as well as intellectual support. It arouses sympathy in observers. At the same time it invites a review of previously held positions on the basis of a clearer view of the truth of the situation. It produces an altered set of circumstances in which attention and action become more irresistibly necessary. Persuasive power is mixed with various elements of pressure. Resisters may win enough public support to coerce diehards in the opposition, or they may succeed in exerting other kinds of nonviolent force, which results in a decisive shift in the balance of power.

Even when these possibilities are not entirely realized, genuine social power is let loose. This is promising enough to call for a great deal more research and experimentation. The method might fill crucial existing gaps in our procedures for social progress. We ought to divert a great deal more study and practice time to understanding and perfecting the process. If we accepted such an agenda for our attention, nonviolent strategies for social conflict might well show as impressive and unbelievable maturing in the future as weapons for physical warfare have had a spectacular development in the past.

This should be of particular concern to the church and to individual churchmen. If the church is to remain faithful to its Lord, it must accept the mission of proclaiming the gospel by word and deed. The worshiping church is also a community of witness and work. A sovereign God, judging every imperfection of finite man, calls his church to activity in the frontier zones of social progress. The use of nonviolent resistance is one of these issues at the cutting edge of thought and practice. If other groups do not sponsor research into its potentialities, the church should encourage such study. If the general public hesitates to experiment with the method, churchmen should set the example.

The church should keep this method also under strict evaluation. Its ethical limitations need to be exposed. Explorations are still called for beyond nonviolent resistance in the direction of a greater expression of "good for evil" and a richer blend of love with coercion. At the same time churchmen should be motivated to more active approval of nonviolent resistance under existing circumstances. As they should be the first to speak against social evil, so they should also be the first to support a better method.

In its own history the church has a long record of nonviolent resistance under persecution. It has often itself become "the suffering seed." Against injustice it has preached the righteousness of nonconformity. The genuine Christian is not an inoffensive little man running from the crowd like a frightened rabbit. The church at its best is not in the business of buying approval from "principalities and powers" by standing as a hindrance to human progress. Nor does it seek to be tolerated and patronized because it has become apathetic and irrelevant. These are temptations to betrayal and apostasy. They would make the church a pathetic anachronism and would lead individual Christians to a life that perjured their protestations to God. The revitalization of the church historically has followed from acceptance of a new revelation of God's truth and power, which it has proclaimed courageously, even within a hostile world. Today new life may again flow through the church only as it responds to the leading of the Holy Spirit in robustly relating pioneering insights to the frontier issues of contemporary life.

These insights and issues are as broad as the total theological and sociological spectrum. A spiritually renewed church will move far beyond interest in any particular method of social change. Yet a more adequate witness about the relationship of love to social strategy is one of the most important frontier needs of our times. A prophetic church will be more seriously interested in the ancient, yet still novel method of nonviolent resistance.

The church should also eagerly appropriate every insight growing out of the analysis of the nonviolent process that relates to the social witness of the church in general. An examination of nonviolent direct action does lead to such a more general understanding of the nature of social progress, and the role of the responsible church. Nonviolent campaigns can teach us much about the more normal and more sustained activities of every creative churchman and responsible citizen. These wider implications now deserve attention.

In the first place, nonviolent resistance reminds us forcefully that apparently insignificant men can have decisive social influence. Resistance movements have demonstrated that the powerless can wield power and that social means can be democratized. The politically subjugated, economically dispossessed, and racially disinherited have accomplished on country roads and city streets what we usually associate only with paneled board rooms and marble legislative halls. One of the chief consequences of resistance campaigns is that they give to disprivileged groups the conviction that there is something they can do about their plight. Nonviolent strategies have given a powerful voice to those otherwise inarticulate. The executives of existing arrangements often assume that those who do not protest are satisfied. This assumption has been shattered by the intensity of feeling breaking through when the silent are given a means for nonviolent expression.

Recent research in related methods shows similar potentialities for the little man. One of the greatest wasted resources of our nation is the citizen power that stays locked up in the masses of the population. Less dramatic forms of interpersonal discussion can build up a powerful public opinion. Even more effective for changing peoples' minds than well-financed campaigns can be the influence of opinion leaders, or persons on all status levels whose judgment is respected by their peers. Studies in group dynamics have indicated that small face-to-face groups can change conduct even more readily than do the mass media. The mood of individual helplessness that permeates our society is unnecessary. If the average citizen lacks power, it is because he has surrendered it by default.

In several respects the church has had long experience in precisely the kinds of procedures that are necessary to revitalize democracy and to increase the individual's actual involvement. In almost every village and neighborhood, churches have small discussion groups meeting regularly. Members are also constantly being trained in evangelistic witness. In our theology of the laity we have emphasized the significance of the common routines of life for committed persons on all status levels. We have stressed that the church is present wherever they work

worthily. All who will listen have been asked to turn their oc-
cupations into vocations. Every man can become a witness for
God. In a nurturing fellowship we have tried to release the
transforming energy latent in the common man.

The church has the essential resources and procedures for a
major impact on social change. It also possesses the basic
theological orientation that is necessary. But it still lacks sufficient program content in this area. More of all these items
could well be used, of course. But to do a thoroughly creditable
job of arousing and informing public opinion, it is not essential
to have any more buildings, any increase in numbers of leaders,
any larger budgets. We need no revisions in Scripture, no different set of basic beliefs, no radical new interpretation of
general ethical position. We do desperately need a sharper
focusing of our strengths on important life issues. A great deal
of talk goes on in churches. Very little of it is careful, detailed
analysis of the cutting edges of Christian witness in the modern
world. We are too traditional, and not contemporary enough.
We are too general, and not specific enough. We deal too much
with easy problems already solved, and too little with the
difficult real dilemmas of man in his vocational and political
life.

From the experience of resistance movements as well as from
related findings in more conventional activities, we can take
new courage. If we can channel the liberated strength of overlooked persons into important issues, we will have developed an
amazing new resource for social improvement and spiritual
growth.

A second illuminating general insight emerges from a study
of the nonviolent process. It concerns the importance of the
middle ranges in the spectrum of public opinion. The swing of
those in the center toward either the resisters or their opponents
to a great extent determines the outcome of a struggle. If any
major social reform in a democracy is to be successful, it must
arouse those who have previously been indifferent and make
them to some degree supporters of the cause. Reformers can-

not wait for those at the opposite extreme to come along. They are too rigid in their opinion. They may be coerced, but they are not likely to be persuaded. It is possible and even necessary to win a campaign while diehards remain of their same contrary opinion.

It is a mistake to direct too much of one's program toward the active opposition and too little toward those in the middle. By paying so much attention to the former, we are aiming at a mirage instead of at the real target. Opponents may win the contest if they can divert enough of the energies of a protest movement against themselves, thus preventing reformers from working at their more important task with less rigid groups.

This is a particular temptation to religious persons, who want to stay on good terms with everyone, either for the sake of loving fellowship or because they take seriously the conversion of all men. Campbell and Pettigrew, in their study of ministers in the Little Rock integration crisis, stated two consequences of toning down one's expression in order to remain on speaking terms with more extreme opponents. "The milder the tone and the less frequent the discussion, the more likely he is to preserve communication with those most distant from his own position. . . . The milder the tone and the less frequent the discussion, the less moral compulsion . . . is felt by a presently unconvinced but pliable group."[4] In other words, in trying to retain communication with those who will not be changed anyway, we neglect the crucial middle group that can be changed. Since we do not arouse opposition from the extremists, we do not awaken support from the moderates. Students of the New Testament should not require sociologists to tell them this. After all, as in his relationship with the Pharisees, Jesus was an expert at winning staunch disciples by enunciating truths that alienated his opponents.

Martin Luther King was similarly troubled by the failure to take a strong stand which, through compromise and delay, effectively removed many men of goodwill from the actual struggle. In his classic "Letter from Birmingham Jail," directed toward fellow clergymen, he wrote:

I must make two honest confessions to you, my Christian and Jewish brothers. First, I must confess that over the past few years I have been gravely disappointed with the white moderate. I have almost reached the regrettable conclusion that the Negro's great stumbling block in his stride toward freedom is not the White Citizen's Counciler or the Ku Klux Klanner but the white moderate who is more devoted to "order" than to justice; who prefers a negative peace which is the absence of tension to a positive peace which is the presence of justice; . . . and who constantly advises the Negro to wait for a "more convenient season." Shallow understanding from people of good will is more frustrating than absolute misunderstanding from people of ill will. Lukewarm acceptance is much more bewildering than outright rejection.[5]

This leads to a third basic insight. Sharp conflict is inevitable in any basic social change. Progress at fundamental points involves shifts in power and privilege. Deep individual and group interests are involved. These are never surrendered easily. Even well-meaning people do not keep moving in the direction of reform unless the discontented keep pushing. When major injustices exist, the absence of visible conflict is not evidence of peace and harmony. It is, rather, an indication of apathy and of the perpetuation of exploitation. Hidden tensions exist so long as injustice continues. These tensions must be brought to the surface before they can be seen and dealt with. Under such circumstances reformers do not so much disturb the peace as that the peace has already been disturbed. "When Ahab saw Elijah, Ahab said to him, 'Is it you, you troubler of Israel?' And he answered, 'I have not troubled Israel; but you have, and your father's house, because you have forsaken the commandments of the Lord'" (I Kings 18:17–18).

Recognition of the role of conflict in basic social change ought to shake our naïve confidence in the complete adequacy of smooth, gradual educational processes. Education is always important. But relying only on calm dialogue, amiable discussion, or unruffled therapy is utopian. This is a sentimental heritage from a shallow liberalism, based on a false view of man. Respectable people, infected with this illusion, are often willing to do anything for a cause except what is necessary to advance it. Their course of action actually becomes immoral because it leaves evil firmly entrenched.

Human nature is considerably more complex than church-men often pretend it to be. Personality develops not only by gradual growth but also through crises. Life is often disorderly rather than neatly organized. Men become sinners as well as saints. Since there are also irrational roots of conduct, un-answerable logic does not constitute a good enough case.

The Bible speaks much of brotherly interaction and orderly enlightenment, but it also gives a place to the seemingly un-couth roughness of Amos or the sharp denunciations of Pharisaism by Jesus. "I have not come to bring peace, but a sword" (Matt. 10:34) recognizes the divisive nature of the gospel. It was rightly said of Jesus, "He is our peace, who has made us both one, and has broken down the dividing wall of hostility" (Eph. 2:14). The reconciling process, however, in-cluded the turbulence of Jerusalem streets and the violence perpetrated on Golgotha. Modern disciples cannot expect to be any more fortunate. There is also a twentieth-century ring about "Do not be surprised at the fiery ordeal which comes upon you" (I Peter 4:12). There is always a cross on the way to redemption.

Churchmen must deal with controversial issues if they expect to affect the future. So long as they speak only about matters of general agreement, they merely reflect what already exists. Whenever they erect a guiding sign at a fork in the road, where mankind is preparing to change direction, they are inevitably involved in controversy about the alternatives. When the choice is a basically important one, that is, when it involves power interests, taking a position always involves ferment, antagonisms, and conflict. In love we try to keep these to a minimum. We do everything possible to approach conflict crea-tively.[6] Yet it is still true that if no one ever leaves a church, the minister is not preaching the gospel. If social action programs do not trigger turbulence, they are not aimed at the really important issues of the time. We cannot escape this. When we try to do so, we become allies of corruption or exploitation.

A fourth major implication of our study points to the importance of the power structures of society. These have been repeatedly neglected by those committed to good social deeds. Idealists have often busied themselves talking to one another or to a few easily made converts around the edges of culture. All the time the major decisions were being made by quite a different group nearer the center of things. Although churchmen might win a few tiny triumphs with occasional persons in the lower ranks of leadership, the main trend of policy has often moved so massively in a contrary direction that they had no chance even to engage in a rearguard skirmish.

Basic decisions in our society are made with disproportionate frequency by a few representatives of great concentrations of power. This is not necessarily sinister or diabolical. To a certain extent this becomes inevitable in a mass society in which town-meeting democracy necessarily must be replaced by representative democracy. So long as representatives remain responsive to the general directions formulated by a ferment of public discussion, there can be little objection. However, those at the peak of major pyramids of power easily undertake to use mass publicity devices to manipulate public opinion to support the decisions they have already made. In any event, whether they are responsive or manipulative, their influence on public decision is always greater than any other group of like size. They cannot be disregarded with impunity. To secure any basic change, especially if it threatens the established distribution of privileges and prerogatives, it is essential that the power elite be persuaded as far as possible and coerced as far as necessary.

Leaders of the church are seldom members of the inner circles of social power. Social scientists are more likely to locate the church as part of the conveyor belt apparatus that interprets centralized decision to the public and solicits popular support. Although this is not always fair to the church, there is enough truth in the picture to startle us into rebellion. Instead of proclaiming the Word of God, we have too often popularized the words of important men.

Our situation is not hopeless. Both churchmen and citizens in general can neutralize or influence the power structures of contemporary society. The church has a long tradition of nonconformity. In its best moments it has always refused to become a stooge for either reformers or exploiters. Only God deserves unvarying obedience. No man qualifies for such consistent allegiance. Our national tradition emphasizes a healthy revolt against autocratic controls. On both religious and political grounds we ought to develop strong defenses against manipulation of opinion from any source. Ours should be a healthy skepticism about all propaganda. Anyone who demands anything approaching a monopoly in publicity ought thereby to be signing a death warrant for his ideas.

Power elites can still be influenced. Sincere laymen may be found among them or may win an accepted status. The church, if it sets itself to the task, may sometimes be able to communicate effectively. After all, it still possesses considerable prestige in our culture. Other organized groups may also exercise a countervailing strength. Small groups and concerned individuals at the bottom can match entrenched power at the top. If necessary, a power base can be developed to force action by the chief decision makers. In the light of scholarly study, however, there is one thing that we can no longer do. Reformers dare not proceed as though concentrations of power did not exist. Adequate planning requires a strategy for dealing with the realistic power factors in our situation.

In a world characterized by such vectors of force, we do well to combine pressure and goodwill. This is a fifth lesson to be learned from nonviolent resisters. Neither naked power nor unimplemented love alone meets the requirements of our existence. As has just been shown, the defense of principle requires prudence regarding power structures. But it is equally true that where coercion must be used, it is best done in an accompanying climate of goodwill.

The converging evidence of various behavioral sciences was earlier referred to in this connection. Disciplines such as educational psychology, criminology, or industrial relations recognize the need for fixing limits, but within a framework of understanding, acceptance, and regard for the legitimate aims of the other. Whenever it seems necessary to spank a child, it is all the more essential that a relationship of affection should have been built up. Much of the unique effectiveness of nonviolent resistance has also been found in this "mix" of ambivalent elements. Resisters have not always been true to their own highest insights on this matter. Furthermore, they have been dealing with a spectrum of subgroups in society, ranging through varying degrees of support and opposition. This differential receptivity has also called for different recipes for compounding the diverse elements in nonviolence. Nevertheless, discussion in earlier chapters has noted, in one form or another, characteristic emphases on firm insistence with a minimum of personal threat, social reform through self-purification, and pressure by suffering.

When action is motivated by love, observers are likely to remain open for more ready acceptance. Even the negative reactions to coercion may be reduced. Therefore whenever it is necessary to use pressure, it is also important to pause to listen to the opponent, to take the trouble to understand, and to find some way to project genuine regard for his legitimate interests. Communication becomes more persuasive if it demonstrates conviction without dogmatism. It is a delicate but desirable balance for a person to search genuinely for larger truth at the same time that he presses for adoption of the truth as he now sees it. He should want less to crush his opponent, and more to contribute to the opponent's growth. If a person regards opponents as devils and treats them accordingly, his is likely to become a self-fulfilling prophecy. It is better, while standing

staunchly for one's position, to see some good in one's antagonist. When a person perceives himself as also part of the sickness
of civilization, a more thorough therapy is likely to be com-
pleted.

The usual etiquette of political and economic conflict does
not provide for this kind of balanced action. At this point even
churchmen have fallen into the ways of this world. Men
typically fear that compassion will be interpreted as weakness,
or that an expression of appreciation might be considered a
concession and might simply invite greater demands for capitulation. Under some circumstances this may temporarily occur,
when relationships have seriously deteriorated or when the
velvet glove too thoroughly hides the iron hand. But we also
know that because parents have spent long hours providing the
needs of the child, because management and labor leaders have
developed rapport, or because the prison social worker has
helped the offender with his personal problems, these persons
have strengthened their positions when it is necessary to draw a
line.

Conflict groups in the community still need to learn this.
The fellowship of the church might well provide a setting for
such lessons. Members of the church who are also members of
opposing social groups can often meet under church auspices—
not only to face "safe" matters unrelated to the conflict but
also to discuss the conflict under circumstances more conducive
to brotherly concern. Or the church in its own social witness
often needs to establish closer relationships with those it criti-
cizes. When admonition of an individual is called for, the
minister should not try to do his pastoral work through a
denunciatory sermon from the pulpit. Neither is it enough for
a denomination in a sheltered meeting to adopt a critical
resolution and hand it to the press. This is about as impersonal
a form of communication as it is possible to devise. It allows
us to denounce gambling without ever meeting the gamblers.
We need to learn to give more concrete expression to the compassion we feel for all groups in society, and especially for those

whose action we oppose or whose position we abhor.

A sixth general insight to emerge from analysis of non-violent resistance is that steady, appropriate, realistic next steps are normally the fastest way to arrive at thoroughgoing change. Resisters are militants in their desire for rapid progress. Nonviolent resistance is most significantly a technique for speeding up change. Yet a certain restraint is seen as preferable to more radical methods which would actually slow down or block improvement.

Resisters involved in difficult campaigns have often proceeded by stages, setting limited goals for specific demonstrations and accepting compromise settlements. Both Gandhi and Southern Negroes, for example, have also allowed rather lengthy intervals between periods of active major resistance. One test of leadership is the ability to determine how much threat or acceleration the situation will bear.

Persistence plus patience is a strange formula for minds that deal in distorted blacks and whites. A thoughtless passion for sudden results often leads to self-defeating violence. It seems obvious to the Neanderthal men among us that the quickest way with opposition is to knock it into line with overwhelming power. According to this view, a child will respond quickly if slapped hard enough. This oversimplified theory overlooks the fact that six months later the child may rebel against every suggestion. Or, in foreign policy, impatient, trigger-happy zealots may want to call out the Marines to crash through every variety of impediment. This easily becomes a stone-ax approach in an environment of delicate electronic machinery. Greater sensitivity to possible dimensions of destruction and to alternative forms of even greater effectiveness would lead us to a more diversified panoply of power. We will get farther faster if we add to responsible military strength such items as skillful negotiation at points of overlapping interest and measures to change the general climate in order that social forces supporting decency and freedom may be gradually strengthened.

In these days of rapid social change we are especially tempted to resort to self-defeating nostrums that actually hinder the very change we want to speed up. It is hard for the utopian to realize that a somewhat slower and more complex immediate approach is often more rapid and simpler in the long run. On the other hand, it is difficult for the realist to see that progress may be too slow and therefore lead to retreat in the long run. Reactionary forces by their noisy criticism or subtle intimidation may not stop progress. If they merely slow it down sufficiently, disaster follows. If right-wing extremists can divert enough creative energy into constant rearguard bickering, both domestic practice and international action will be slowed to such a pace as to make inevitable the spread of totalitarianism and the outbreak of war. This makes it all the more essential that we become adept at the methods that will in the long run prove to be most rapid.

This points toward still another general lesson to be learned from nonviolent resisters. We need to engage more habitually in strenuous programs going beyond our usual verbalization. The essence of nonviolent resistance is unaccustomed nonconformity. It would be unfruitful continuously to practice such a degree of difference. Even during appropriate times for demonstrations, we will not all necessarily sit-in at the lunch counters. "There are varieties of working, but it is the same God who inspires them all." (I Cor. 12:6.) Reform movements need both moderates and militants. Yet it is a mistake to think that moderates can do it alone, especially when power interests are involved. Especially in dynamic times comparatively more militants are needed, along with comparatively fewer moderates. Against tough opposition it is essential to go beyond everyday methods. Drawing up petitions in support of forlorn causes may become a useless pastime. A more novel initiative and a more intense enthusiasm are required.

Writing about the American South, Merrill Proudfoot said, "At our campus church this morning, 'Stay Away from Downtown' leaflets were passed out with the Communion bulletins."[7] Christians should come to see this not as a jarring contrast, but

as a uniquely compatible combination. The church by its tim-
idity and rigidity has often remained a sixteenth-century enclave
in a twentieth-century world.

We have noted how a nonviolence campaign may shatter
superficial contacts, but then, after a period of conflict and division, move into a more genuine dialogue characterized by
deeper workings of the Spirit. The church operates too con-
sistently on the level of shallow relationships. We claim too
much for our usual talk. We regard ourselves as being prophetic
when we oppose racial segregation in those communities in
which both political parties and most national newsmagazines
also oppose segregation. Or we claim to be courageous in speaking favorably of the United Nations when polls show that over
90 percent of the American people are favorably disposed to
the United Nations. The church had better not claim the
heritage of the prophets when it only makes a few slightly
stimulating noises. Nor has its ministry communicated anything
when it merely repeats safe generalizations that the congrega-
tion once again accepts without any fresh thought. Much talk
about high principles still leaves hearers wallowing in their
bland and blank inertia.

There are narrower limits to the kind of action appropriate
to the church as an organization than to the individual churchman. Yet both can go far beyond verbalization. To be sure, we
act when we speak. But we also speak through other forms of
action. The church has engaged in this propaganda of the deed
in its various social welfare programs, in hospitals or recreation
centers or agricultural demonstrations. What are counterparts
for this in social reform? At least there are novel places to
speak, as before legislative committees or in reform organizations. There are also other forms of action, like demonstrations,
the organization of alternative social structures, or the layman's
witness in his vocational conduct.

If we take this matter seriously, the theological education of
ministers and the continuing reading of ministers and laymen
will be considerably altered. For adequacy in our culture a wider

range of competence is required in religion just as it is in other fields. Many details of traditional subjects are no longer germane to present requirements. They have become pedantic rather than scholarly. They ought to be replaced in our study by more relevant materials, particularly now from the behavioral sciences and the arts.

Before religion can make its indispensable modern impact, the prevailing image of ministerial success must also be altered. (A comparable shift in definition is required of laymen. Furthermore, laymen are largely responsible for the prevailing image of the successful minister.) Contradictory expectations concerning his role place the minister in a difficult dilemma. Congregations, ecclesiastical leaders, and even ministers themselves, when they are making actual evaluations of church leaders, seem predominantly to judge them in terms of institutional criteria. A minister is considered successful if he has increased membership, buildings, and financial support. As Pettigrew and Campbell suggested, "However exalted the moral virtue the minister expounds, the hierarchy does not wish him to damn his listeners to Hell unless somehow he gets them back in time to attend service each Sunday."[8] On the other hand, when role expectations are more theoretically or theologically discussed, temporary losses of membership are not considered such great calamities. The prophetic function looms larger. Courageous leadership in spiritual growth and community change then becomes an important criterion. Until the theological becomes the operational image also of the successful minister, we can expect little vigorous leadership from the church.

This generation's picture of "religion that is pure and undefiled" (James 1:27) needs refurbishing. Does faith most characteristically support men in unusual steps toward social improvement? Or is it more likely to motivate those who protect existing order in spite of underlying injustices? Police Commissioner Eugene Conner, watching Birmingham Negroes in mass demonstration, remarked, "Boy, if that's religion, I don't want any."[9] After a Negro leader, Rev. Fred L. Shuttlesworth, had been pinned against the side of a church by a fire hose and carried away on a stretcher in an ambulance, Commissioner Conner was quoted as saying, "I wish they'd carried him away in a hearse."[10] One might properly reply to that statement, "Sir, if that's religion, I don't want any."

When justice waits to be won, the New Testament faith is more authentically expressed by marching into fire hoses than by wishing that protest leaders were embalmed in a hearse. If more church members, as a consequence of righteous demonstration, were physically lying on ambulance stretchers, the church might experience a remarkable spiritual revitalization.

A last general contribution of an analysis of nonviolent resistance grows out of its emphasis on the transforming power of voluntary suffering. This is one of the more ultimate resources in heroic love. It emerges only when willing the good for the neighbor is pushed to the point that it becomes costly. Suffering accompanies the fullest expression of love. This kind of love goes beyond mutuality, which makes an equal claim for self and for another. When one suffers, he has given priority to the needs of neighbor over his own needs. In social struggle, this involves giving preference even to the needs of the opponent. The Gospel of John includes the observation, "Greater love has no man than this, that a man lay down his life for his friends" (John 15:13). Yet there is a more radical love. The statement in John is to be amended with the spirit of Jesus expressed in "Love your enemies, do good to those who hate you, bless those who curse you, pray for those who abuse you" (Luke 6:27–28). In the light of this, there is no greater love than laying down one's life for one's enemies. It is hard to see how love could be pushed any farther. This is the quality which is approximated in any serious suffering of genuinely nonviolent and compassionate resisters.

To be sure, this is only one element in nonviolent resistance. For reasons that have already been fully indicated, the limitations of an imperfect situation necessitate a more complex strategy than simply suffering. In this complexity is to be found part of the strength of the method. Yet it has also been previously shown that the element of suffering involved is likewise a form of practical power. When an adequate place has been given to coercion as a factor in the success of a nonviolence campaign, it is still true that suffering has demonstrated an additional important persuasive consequence. Social influence is exerted by the right kind of loving action. It is possible to win by what appears to be one's own defeat. Victory may become more likely through accepting pain.

Persuasion, negotiation, political action, and economic pressure are still the basic nonviolent methods to be relied upon for social change. Only infrequently will these be pushed to such lengths of unconventionality as to result in dramatic suffering. Yet at all times, these four general methods will be more adequate if they are inspired by a love willing to suffer. The pain actually imposed upon us may involve only the minor inconveniences of absorbing time and energy, or the surrender of some forms of social advancement, or the personal tensions of social controversy. Even so, our willingness to accept these may make the difference between creative contribution and futile gesture, and between obedience and rebellion toward God.

Although these supportive attitudes are necessary to keep our methods most effective, they are nevertheless very much in short supply. The strategies of love are only imperfectly known. The cultural ideal of our time seems to embody more of aggressive, egoistic domination of others than it includes persistent, altruistic spending of self. A moderate measure of suffering for the sake of others is accepted as part of our image of parenthood. The quality is quite obscured, however, in commonly accepted economic and political roles. Even while we are working toward generally good ends, we want to protect our comfort in the process.

Both Biblical and sociological insight suggest that we ought to be more ready to embody sacrificial elements in all of our daily social interaction. In an unjust world we cannot escape the displeasure of the protectors of wickedness. Affluence cannot shield us from it. Since evil always resists eradication, progress is impossible without pain. Whenever in social reform it seems possible to sidestep suffering, we had better be suspicious of that alternative, lest it be a rationalization of selfish desire. In an imperfect world the burden of proof is on the side of the placid life. When one of the colonial Quakers, Mary Dyer, was already standing on the gallows and was then reprieved at the last moment, she felt "disturbed." She hesitated to obey the command to step down, for she wanted to wait on the Lord "to know his pleasure in so sudden a change."[11] Were we more deeply dedicated, we would more often hesitate to escape from perilous testimony.

A wider experience of suffering love would also help us deal with the finitude, anxiety, and estrangement of man on more profound levels than social reform. Significance and meaning for life emerge from utter absorption in greater goals outside oneself. We are rescued from superficial, casual contacts by genuine, self-giving relationships. A view of life in depth uncovers grounds for hope before which lesser threats become trivial. The emptiness of hollow men can be filled by a transforming devotion to God and neighbor. "He who loses his life for my sake will find it." (Matt. 10:39.) Suffering for compassionate ends is transmuted into spiritual growth and the fulfillment of the highest purposes of existence.

This is rooted much more deeply than our involvement in human relationships. If we believe that God exhibits love carried to the point of the cross, then this becomes the character of the basic relationship of reality. God's initiative of sacrificial love moves us to introduce larger measures of love into our own lives. The consequence and test for knowing God is the depth of our actual love for men. "He who does not love does not know God; for God is love. . . . He who abides in love abides in God, and God abides in him." (I John 4:8, 16.) "By this we know love, that he laid down his life for us; and we ought to lay down our lives for the brethren." (I John 3:16.)

It is not that we ought somehow to alter the nature of the

universe in order to make love to the uttermost the last word about life. Love is already that last word. God steadfastly loves us far beyond our understanding. It is for us to accept that fact and so to respond that the nature of our human association may be decisively altered. Far deeper than man's fragile conquest of any specific injustice lies God's mighty empowering of new persons in transforming relationships of more vital love.

NOTES

Chapter 1.   Distinctive Features of a Novel Method

1. Leslie W. Dunbar, executive director of the Southern Regional Council, in *New South,* July–August, 1961, p. 9.

2. Karl Mannheim, *Diagnosis of Our Time* (Oxford University Press, Inc., 1944), p. 13.

3. Krishnalal Shridharani, *War Without Violence: A Study of Gandhi's Method and Its Accomplishments* (Harcourt, Brace and World, Inc., 1939), p. 5.

4. It should be noted that nonviolent resistance and nonviolent direct action are here used synonymously. Attempted distinctions between the two terms tend to break down. Nonviolent resistance is here given the preferred usage, because it is the traditional, simpler, and more widely used term. There has been some tendency recently to use "nonviolence" to designate the method. The meaning commonly communicated by this term, however, covers far too much territory.

5. Joan V. Bondurant, *Conquest of Violence: The Gandhian Philosophy of Conflict* (Princeton University Press, 1958), p. 103.

6. Martin Luther King, Jr., *Stride Toward Freedom: The Montgomery Story* (Ballantine Books, Inc., 1958), p. 111.

7. *Speeches and Writings of Mahatma Gandhi,* 4th ed. (Madras: G. H. Natesan & Co., 1933), p. 346.

8. Gandhi, "The Running Sore," *Young India,* August 8, 1929, p. 263.

9. Quoted in Gopi Nath Dhawan, *The Political Philosophy of Mahatma Gandhi,* 3d rev. ed. (Ahmedabad: Navajivan Publishing House, 1957), p. 52.

10. George Bishop, *New England Judged by the Spirit of the Lord,* 2d ed. (London: T. Sowle, 1703), pp. 241–242.

11. Joseph Besse, *A Collection of the Sufferings of the People*

Called Quakers (London: Luke Hinde, 1753), Vol. 2, p. 264.

12. New York *Times*, March 6, 1919, p. 10.

13. Muriel Lester, "Gandhi—World Citizen," *motive*, December, 1949, p. 7.

14. *Speeches and Writings of Mahatma Gandhi*, p. 470.

15. C. F. Andrews, *Mahatma Gandhi, His Own Story* (The Macmillan Company, 1930), p. 330.

16. Bondurant, *op. cit.*, p. 22.

17. *Speeches and Writings of Mahatma Gandhi*, pp. 659–660.

18. M. K. Gandhi, *Non-Violent Resistance (Satyagraha)*, ed. by Bharatan Kumarappa (Schocken Books, Inc., 1961), p. 315.

19. *Ibid.*, p. 323.

20. C. F. Andrews, *Mahatma Gandhi's Ideas* (The Macmillan Company, 1930), p. 366.

21. Dhawan, *op. cit.*, p. 139.

22. Doris Stevens, *Jailed for Freedom* (Boni & Liveright, 1920), p. 16.

Chapter 2.   Division and Conflict in the Resistance Process

1. "War-Time Offenders Out of Jail," *Literary Digest*, December 11, 1920, p. 20.

2. Ray H. Abrams, *Preachers Present Arms* (Round Table Press, Inc., 1933), pp. 131–142, 147–152.

3. Anna Holden, "A First Step Toward School Integration" (Congress of Racial Equality, 1958), p. 5.

4. King, *Stride Toward Freedom*, pp. 98–102; L. D. Reddick, *Crusader Without Violence* (Harper & Row, Publishers, Inc., 1959), pp. 171–173.

5. A. K. Jameson and Gene Sharp, "Non-Violent Resistance and the Nazis: The Case of Norway," in Mulford Q. Sibley, ed., *The Quiet Battle* (Doubleday & Company, Inc., 1963), pp. 164–165, 170–186.

6. Thomas Gaither, "Behind the Carolina Stockade," *Social Progress*, February, 1961, p. 12.

7. Bishop, *op. cit.*, pp. 403 ff.

8. *Ibid.*, p. 319.

9. *Ibid.*, p. 342.

10. *Speeches and Writings of Mahatma Gandhi*, p. 473.

11. *Ibid.*

12. Inez H. Irwin, *The Story of the Woman's Party* (Harcourt, Brace & World, Inc., 1921), p. 472.

13. New York *Times*, November 11, 1917, I, pp. 1, 3.

14. *Ibid.,* November 13, 1917, p. 4.
15. *Ibid.,* November 14, 1917, p. 6.
16. Massachusetts Historical Society, *Collections,* Series 4, Vol. 9, p. 158.
17. Donald W. Riddle, *The Martyrs: A Study in Social Control* (The University of Chicago Press, 1931), p. 83.
18. Bishop, *op. cit.,* pp. 476–477.
19. Vincent Harding and Staughton Lynd, "Albany, Georgia," *Crisis,* February, 1963, p. 73.
20. Washington *Herald,* November 5, 1917, p. 1.

Chapter 3.   Resolution and Reconciliation in the Resistance Process

1. Shridharani, *op. cit.,* pp. 36–37.
2. *Ibid.,* p. 40.
3. *Ibid.,* p. 37. For similar reactions to the early Christian martyrs, see C. J. Cadoux, *The Early Church and the World* (Edinburgh: T. & T. Clark, 1925), pp. 220–221.
4. Negley Farson in Eugene Lyons, ed., *We Cover the World* (Harcourt, Brace and World, Inc., 1937), p. 143.
5. Gene Sharp, *Gandhi Wields the Weapon of Moral Power* (Ahmedabad: Navajivan Publishing House, 1960), p. 166.
6. *Suffragist,* February 9, 1918, p. 9.
7. Stevens, *op. cit.,* pp. 158–163; New York *Times,* September 8, 1917, pp. 1, 3.
8. New York *Times,* August 9, 1918, p. 10.
9. *Suffragist,* July 21, 1917, p. 10.
10. Washington *Herald,* July 2, 1917, p. 1; *Suffragist,* November 17, 1917, p. 8.
11. Washington *Herald,* August 15, 1917, p. 6.
12. Bishop, *op. cit.,* pp. 10–11, 61–62, 89–92.
13. Samuel Deane, *History of Scituate* (James Loring, 1831), pp. 371–372.
14. Bishop, *op. cit.,* p. 60; Humphrey Norton, *New England's Ensigne* (London: G. Calvert, 1659), p. 72.
15. Besse, *op. cit.,* Vol. 2, p. 238.
16. N. B. Shurtleff, ed., *Records of the Governor and Company of the Massachusetts Bay in New England* (William White, 1853–1854), Vol. 4 (1), pp. 383–384.
17. Los Angeles *Times,* July 14, 1963, p. A.
18. Martin Smolin, " 'We Walk So They May Sit,' " *Social Progress,* February, 1961, p. 17.

19. *New South,* July–August, 1961, p. 9.

20. *The Freedom Ride* (Southern Regional Council, a "special report" issued in May, 1961), p. 6.

21. Edward A. Ross in Introduction to Clarence Marsh Case, *Non-Violent Coercion: A Study in Methods of Social Pressure* (The Century Company, 1923), no page number.

22. "World Press Views Freedom Rides and the United States," *New South,* July–August, 1961, pp. 14–15.

23. New York *Times,* January 17, 1917, p. 7.

24. *Ibid.,* February 5, 1919, p. 18.

25. *Suffragist,* February 16, 1918, p. 14.

26. Frederick B. Fisher, *That Strange Little Brown Man Gandhi* (Long and Smith, 1932), p. 159.

27. Reddick, *op. cit.,* pp. 228–229.

28. John Norton, *The Heart of New-England Rent at the Blasphemies of the Present Generation* (London: John Allen, 1660), pp. 2, 6–7, 40; Cotton Mather, *Magnalia Christi Americana* (Silas Andrus, 1820), Vol. 1, p. 444, and Vol. 2, pp. 452, 454, 456–458; John Hull, *Diaries,* in American Antiquarian Society, *Transactions and Collections* (J. Wilson, 1857), Vol. 3, p. 202; Shurtleff, ed., *op. cit.,* Vol. 4 (1), pp. 386–387.

29. *Speeches and Writings of Mahatma Gandhi,* pp. 197–198.

30. R. R. Diwakar, *Satyagraha: Its Technique and History* (Bombay: Hind Kitabs, 1946), pp. 53–54.

31. Farson in Lyons, ed., *op. cit.,* pp. 137–138.

32. Aage Bertelsen, *October '43* (G. P. Putnam's Sons, 1954), p. 135.

33. Richard B. Gregg, *The Power of Non-Violence,* rev. ed. (Fellowship Publications, 1944), pp. 43–44.

34. Nicolas Berdyaev, *The Destiny of Man,* 4th ed. (London: Geoffrey Bles, Ltd., 1954), p. 292.

35. Gene Sharp (in *Nonviolent Action* [London: Friends Peace Committee, n.d.], p. 9) and George Lakey (in *The Sociological Mechanisms of Nonviolent Action* [mimeographed M.A. thesis, submitted to the University of Pennsylvania, 1962], pp. 23 and 34–36), each suggests a third category ("accommodation" and "persuasion," respectively) in addition to "conversion" and "coercion." Their third categories, however, would seem to fall under the heading of coercion, since opponents continue to disagree with resisters on the central point at issue in the conflict. Opponents act in support of the resisters because another factor, different from the point at issue, has been given greater weight than the central point of conflict. This is the essence of

coercion. Another illustration of the reluctance of students friendly to nonviolent resistance to admit its coercive quality can be found in Shridharani, *op. cit.*, pp. 293–294. He attempts a distinction between "compulsion" and "coercion," attributing only the first to Gandhi's method. Not only is this logically unconvincing but, as will be shown in Chapter 4, it is ethically misguided. One can admit coercive elements in nonviolent resistance without thereby lowering one's estimate of the method in contemporary social struggles. William Robert Miller recognizes coercive elements in nonviolent resistance, but his treatment of definitions (*Nonviolence: A Christian Interpretation* [Association Press, 1964, Chs. 1 to 3]), is also marred by an unsatisfactory attempt to place a poorly defined category of "pressure" between persuasion and coercion. He also makes inadequate distinctions between passive resistance and nonviolent direct action, and between violence and coercion. His definition of violence is so broad as to include elements of psychological or spiritual violence in *non*violent resistance.

36. Merrill Proudfoot, *Diary of a Sit-In* (The University of North Carolina Press, 1962), p. 185.

37. Martin Luther King, Jr., "Letter from Birmingham Jail," *The Christian Century*, June 12, 1963, p. 768.

38. *Time*, January 3, 1964, p. 15.

39. B. Pattabhi Sitaramayya, *Gandhi and Gandhiism* (Allahabad: Kitabistan, 1942), Vol. 1, p. 139.

40. William F. Poole, "The Quaker Invasion of Massachusetts," *The Dial*, June, 1883, p. 35.

Chapter 4.   The Ethics of Social Strategy

1. Farson in Lyons, ed., *op. cit.*, p. 137.

2. *Moral Responsibility and United States Power* (Federal Council of Churches, 1949), p. 3.

3. For a stimulating discussion of such antinomies of value, see Nicolai Hartmann, *Ethics* (London: George Allen and Unwin, Ltd., 1932), Vol. 2, pp. 75–122.

4. Harvey Seifert, "A Christian Reappraisal of Realism in Foreign Policy," *Religion in Life*, Winter 1959–1960, reprinted in Donald Keys, ed., *God and the H-Bomb* (Random House, Inc., 1961).

5. *Young India*, August 11, 1920, p. 711.

6. Pyarelal, "An Interlude at Santiniketan," *Harijan*, March 9, 1940, p. 31.

7. Gandhi, "Religion vs. No Religion," *Harijan,* June 9, 1946, p. 172. Cf. Gandhi, "The Monkey Nuisance," *Harijan,* May 5, 1946.

8. *Harijan,* July 7, 1946, p. 213.

9. Pyarelal, *loc. cit.*

10. Gandhi, "My Idea of a Police Force," *Harijan,* September 1, 1940, p. 265.

11. Dhawan, *op. cit.,* p. 68.

12. Gandhi, "How Can Violence Be Stopped?" *Harijan,* May 19, 1946, p. 140.

13. Gandhi, "Religion vs. No Religion," *Harijan,* June 9, 1946, p. 172.

14. Dhawan, *op. cit.,* p. 51.

15. Pyarelal, *loc. cit.*

16. For a good discussion of this essential element in coercion, based on Durkheim's thought, see Talcott Parsons, *The Structure of Social Action* (McGraw-Hill Book Company, Inc., 1937), pp. 378–390.

Chapter 5.   An Evaluation of Nonviolent Resistance

1. "The Albany Story," *Christian Advocate,* September 27, 1962, pp. 23–24.

2. Alan B. Anderson, in "The Albany Story," *loc. cit.,* p. 24.

3. Jawaharlal Nehru, *An Autobiography* (London: John Lane, 1936), pp. 539, 540.

4. K. G. Mashruwala in preface to Diwakar, *op. cit.,* p. xiv.

5. Reinhold Niebuhr, *Moral Man and Immoral Society* (Charles Scribner's Sons, 1932), p. 20.

6. Nehru, *op. cit.,* p. 551.

7. Arnold Toynbee, "How to Change the World Without War," *Saturday Review,* May 12, 1962, p. 49.

8. Los Angeles *Times,* December 21, 1954.

9. In Quincy Wright, William M. Evan, and Morton Deutsch, eds., *Preventing World War III: Some Proposals* (Simon and Schuster, Inc., 1962), pp. 213–225. One of the earlier publications of the article was in *The Christian Century,* May 2, 1951.

10. S. Radhakrishnan, ed., *Mahatma Gandhi: Essays and Reflections on His Life and Work,* 2d ed. (London: George Allen and Unwin, Ltd., 1949), p. 282.

11. Shridharani, *op. cit.,* p. 22.

12. Bishop, *op. cit.,* p. 336.

13. Norton, *op. cit.,* p. 72; Besse, *op. cit.,* Vol. 2, p. 184.

14. James Peck, *Freedom Ride* (Simon and Schuster, Inc., 1962), p. 57.

15. King, *Stride Toward Freedom*, p. 132.

16. Dhawan, *op. cit.*, p. 135.

17. *Ibid.*

18. *Harijan*, February 1, 1935, p. 410.

19. For an effective fictional presentation, see George Orwell, *Nineteen Eighty-Four* (Harcourt, Brace and World, Inc., 1949).

20. Stephen King-Hall, *Defense in the Nuclear Age* (Fellowship Publications, 1959), pp. 209–216.

21. Dhawan, *op. cit.*, p. 163.

22. Andrews, *Mahatma Gandhi's Ideas*, p. 144.

23. *Ibid.*, p. 192.

24. Lerone Bennett, Jr., "What Sit-downs Mean to America," *Social Progress*, February, 1961, p. 26. Reprinted from *Ebony*, June, 1960.

25. Radhakrishnan, ed., *op. cit.*, pp. 281–282.

26. *The Freedom Ride* (Southern Regional Council, a "special report" issued in May, 1961), pp. 4–5.

Chapter 6.   A Realistic View of the Limitations of Nonviolence

1. *Young India*, March 20, 1930, p. 103.

2. Dhawan, *op. cit.*, p. 75.

3. Martin Luther King, Jr., *Strength to Love* (Harper & Row, Publishers, Inc., 1963), p. 40.

4. M. Abdul Qadir Kasuri, "Non-violence at Peshawar," *Young India*, May 8, 1930, p. 170.

5. Manabendra Nath Roy, *The Aftermath of Non-cooperation* (London, 1925), p. 114.

6. Aurobindo Ghose, *The Doctrine of Passive Resistance* (Calcutta: Arya Publishing House, 1948), p. 65.

7. Sitaramayya, *op. cit.*, Vol. 1, p. 164.

8. K. G. Mashruwala in preface to Diwakar, *op. cit.*, p. ix.

9. *Ibid.*

10. Lewis A. Coser, "The Termination of Conflict," *Journal of Conflict Resolution*, December, 1961, p. 349.

11. Bishop, *op. cit.*, pp. 431–432, 376–377, 490–491. As a further illustration of similar occasional protests against slavery, see John Greenleaf Whittier's introduction to *The Journal of John Woolman* (Friends' Book Store, 1871), pp. 13–15.

12. Mulford Q. Sibley and Philip E. Jacob, *Conscription of Conscience: The American State and the Conscientious Ob-*

jector, 1940–1947 (Cornell University Press, 1952), pp. 401–410.

13. Nehru, *op. cit.*, p. 554.

14. Miller, *op. cit.*, p. 136.

15. Stevens, *op. cit.*, p. 326.

16. New York *Times,* February 10, 1919, p. 4.

17. For a stimulating discussion of such questions, see Miller, *op. cit.*, Chs. 6 and 7.

18. Quoted in Dhawan, *op. cit.*, p. 331.

19. Devere Allen, "Pacifism and Small Nations," *Fellowship,* February, 1937, p. 4.

20. King-Hall, *op. cit.*, p. 200. For a stimulating discussion of the problem of nonviolent resistance to invasion, see pp. 191–205 of this book by a British military officer.

21. Dhawan, *op. cit.*, p. 270.

22. Mahadev Desai, "The Hour of Trial," *Harijan,* November 4, 1939, p. 331.

23. Pyarelal, "Non-Violence and World Crisis," *Harijan,* December 24, 1938, pp. 394–395.

24. André Trocme, "The Stages of Nonviolence," *Fellowship,* October, 1953, p. 9.

25. Gene Sharp, "Strategic Problems of the South African Resistance," *Peace News,* July 5, 1963, p. 10.

26. Paul Diesing, "Bargaining Strategy and Union-Management Relationships," *Journal of Conflict Resolution,* December, 1961.

27. Karl Barth and Johannes Hamel, *How to Serve God in a Marxist Land* (Association Press, 1959), p. 99. See also the rest of this book and Charles C. West, *Communism and the Theologians* (The Westminster Press, 1958).

Chapter 7. Suffering Love as Social Strategy

1. Jerome D. Frank in Wright, Evan, and Deutsch, eds., *op. cit.*, p. 203, suggests that under some circumstances only the military could lead a resistance movement. If used against dictators occupying one's country, nonviolent resistance would require a highly disciplined organization, diffused leadership, and carefully protected clandestine lines of communication. Frank points out that the armed forces would probably be the only group sufficiently organized and disciplined to lead the country in this form of combat. This suggests further grounds for military interest in nonviolent resistance. However, military leadership might well be temperamentally unsuited and un-

available for such a leadership task. Presumably an invading power would give high priority to decimating and immobilizing military leaders.

2. George F. Kennan, *Russia, the Atom and the West* (Harper & Row, Publishers, Inc., 1957), p. 63.

3. B. H. Liddell Hart, *Deterrent or Defense* (Frederick A. Praeger, Inc., 1960), p. 220.

4. Ernest Q. Campbell and Thomas F. Pettigrew, *Christians in Racial Crisis: A Study of Little Rock's Ministry* (Public Affairs Press, 1959), p. 105.

5. King, "Letter from Birmingham Jail," *loc. cit.,* p. 770.

6. For suggestions, see Ch. 4 in Harvey Seifert, *The Church in Community Action* (Abingdon-Cokesbury Press, 1952).

7. Proudfoot, *op. cit.,* p. 115.

8. Campbell and Pettigrew, *op. cit.,* p. 90.

9. New York *Times,* Western Edition, May 7, 1963, p. 6.

10. *Ibid.,* May 8, 1963, p. 5.

11. Bishop, *op. cit.,* pp. 134–135.

INDEX